EARLY PRAISE FOR

A VOICE FROM HEAVEN

"…**captivates the reader with its powerful and eloquent writing**. The authors fearlessly delve into unexplored territory, offering **a rare glimpse into the intricate concepts that shape our world and the world beyond. Prepare to be moved.** The authors challenge the reader to rethink what the afterlife and eternal life mean." **Penfold reviewer**

"This book gives **profound insights into the nature of existence beyond the physical world, painting a vivid picture of the afterlife and a glimpse into the love and connection that transcends death**. My experience with the book has been **transformative** - I have gained profound insights into the afterlife and the eternal nature of the soul. The authors' own journey of self-discovery and spiritual awakening, seeking guidance from their divine selves and spirit guides, has inspired me to embark on my own spiritual path." **J Chiomaa**

"A titillating, emotional, and extravagant view of the afterlife, human purpose, love, family, and life. It **rattles the cages of what we know life to be** and forces us to examine our preconceived notions of what the afterlife could be. I found myself enthralled from start to finish. It captivated me in such a way that I lost myself in all the possibilities of the world, the afterlife, and life beyond the realm humans can perceive. **I'm transfixed**, and my beliefs have been radically shaken. I've been **left with a soothing feeling of having glimpsed profound knowledge** upon finishing this book. The vivid pictures they construct of the landscape of Heaven and the resounding peace, love, hope, and transcendent being that it showers are beyond simple words, yet they did **such great work conveying them that one could feel them resonating off the pages.**" **Tshepsyt**

"A profoundly moving narrative that explores the realms of life, death, and the afterlife. The message of love, acceptance, and self-discovery is comforting and inspiring. Alec's wisdom shines through as he encourages his mother to embrace life fully and let go of fear and grief. These **messages are powerful and resonate with readers who may be seeking solace and meaning in their own lives.**" **V Kant**

"The **reflections on the "other world" are striking and enchanting. It's a very beautiful and heartwarming story** and testimony, narrated with respect and a great sense of love." **A Perez**

"…it **invites readers to contemplate the mysteries of existence with an open mind**. In terms of impact, "A Voice from Heaven" succeeds in opening up a dialogue about the mysteries of existence and the potential for communication beyond the physical realm. It encourages readers to contemplate their own beliefs about life, death, and what might lie beyond. I would recommend it to those seeking a thought-provoking exploration of life's enigmatic questions." **SuCha**

"A heartfelt and insightful book that offers a unique perspective on the afterlife and our connections to loved ones who have passed on. …the book an engaging and **thought-provoking read, sure to inspire reflection, hope, and a deeper understanding of the mysteries of life and death.**" **A Karmakar**

"I was engaged in reading this book the entire time. - **I couldn't put it down.**" **KDV**

"The author's writing skills shine through the story, which is masterfully woven with a rich tapestry of emotions and vivid descriptions that allow readers to step into the mother's shoes, experiencing her longing and unyielding resolve to communicate with her son. **A tale of hope, it conveys the powerful message that love is capable of transcending the boundary between life and death. It echoes the sentiment that love endures indefinitely, unbroken by the passage from this world to the next. Touches the heart deeply.** Whether one has experienced the loss of a cherished individual or contemplated the mysteries that follow our earthly existence, this book invites readers to reflect profoundly and feel the emotions it evokes." **WAJIDA**

"We have all experienced loss, and we end up with a lot of unanswered questions about what the afterlife is. This book has an answer to those questions. It was written in Alec's voice, and this helps one connect with the

love and peace he felt whenever he talked about heaven. **I was captivated.** I would definitely recommend this book to anyone who, at any point in time, experienced the loss of a loved one and is filled with a lot of questions, or is curious about the afterlife." **Ojukotimi**

"**Mind-blowing revelations** that transcend what we know of spirituality coupled with a grief-stricken yet awe-inspiring passage of a beloved son to the afterlife. These pages may well contain secrets that complement instead of confound a multitude of religions and spiritualities, revealing **more than one "ah-ha" moment.** Not only is this journey one that you'll **not be able to put down,** it's one **you'll never forget.**" R Leahy

"This precious book **brings shivers of familiarity and reason for hope** to anyone whose loved one has passed or suffers from disease, addiction or mental health illness. You can almost feel the anticipatory grief in the parents' journey, then the hope of the afterlife is palpable. A son and his mother connect beyond time and space to share one thing more clearly, more fully, than they ever could in physical life – Love." **B Gornet**

" Following the drug-induced death of her brilliant young son, the author recounts a mother's **spiritual journey to a place of comfort, peace, and love,** made possible by a telepathic connection with her son, who revealed **beautiful images of heaven and assurance of his personal well-being** in the afterlife." **J Evans**

"A mother's cathartic confessional of her unrelenting quest to make peace with her son's unexpected passing. **Gut-wrenchingly honest, bravely depicted,** and painful at times, her child's years-long drug use and ultimate death is disturbing, yet poignant reading. The author's interpretations of the afterlife is **provocative food for thought.** The book's unspoken call to action is: *Forgive, as God forgives us. God is Love; therefore, seek God.*" **N Nuñez**

" A Voice from Heaven is a **captivating book about Love and the beauty of heaven**. This book is a gift to those who have suffered the tragic loss of a loved one." **E Lucius**

"This is a **beautiful story of tragedy and loss, love and faith, and the magic of discovering the afterlife**. After the devastating death of her son, a grieving mother finds solace through a spiritual connection with him. **Their journey together is one of love and learning.**" **K Harris**

A VOICE FROM HEAVEN

From Earthly Struggles to Thriving in the Afterlife

ALEXANDER V. GIRMAN
& CYNTHIA J. GIRMAN

Wings of Peace
PRESS

CYNTHIA J. GIRMAN
avoicefromheaven2023@gmail.com
http://www.wingsofpeacepress.com

Printed Worldwide
First Printing 2023
First Edition 2023

ISBN – Hardcover : 979-8-9882109-0-0
ISBN - Paperback: 979-8-9882109-1-7
ISBN - eBook: 979-8-9882109-2-4
Library of Congress Control Number: 2023936652

Cover Illustration by Stefan Senna
Cover Design by Sallie Williams

DEDICATION

This book was authored by, and is dedicated to, our son, Alexander (Alec) V. Girman, who died much too early for our family, and whom we miss every single day.

And to my daughter and Alec's sister, Vera. You are strong, brave, and confident, with a fabulous mind and view of the world. We hope you always stay true to yourself.

Finally, to all the men and women who suffer from the binds of substance use disorder. May you find the road to recovery and a treatment combination that works for you to ease your pain and allow you to enjoy your natural physical life.

Table of Contents

PROLOGUE

I didn't know I was going to write this book until a few days before I started, and I was surprised every single day when words flowed out of me. I am truly grateful for this astonishing experience, and it has helped me heal.

It is worth noting that I have been a Christian my entire life and grew up very active in the Methodist church. I am not an over-zealous religious fanatic. I don't quote scripture or post 'Praise God!' on social media, and I don't align with evangelists. From that perspective, the messages in this book are surprising and not exactly what I had expected. This book is intended for anyone that believes in a higher power, even though it has some passages that align with Christianity and other passages which may not.

An early reader told me that this book sparks hope in a difficult world, comfort for those who mourn, and mercy and compassion for those with substance use disorders, or who are on the autism spectrum. I hope other readers of the book feel the same. This book does not endorse attempts to join the afterlife sooner than was intended (prematurely ending one's life or suicide). On the contrary, all of us need to live out our journey and purpose in this life. This book is intended to give hope instead of fear for when we pass naturally, at the intended time, as we have much to learn and experience.

This book is written predominantly in Alec's voice. To facilitate clarity, the beginning of each chapter specifies whose voice the chapter is written in, and when Alec starts communicating, it states *Alec's voice*. Any questions that I have for Alec after his voice is introduced are in quotes to distinguish my voice from his.

I hope you, as a reader, gain some understanding from these words, and that they bring peace, no matter what your circumstances may be. May we all strive to know our true inner self and love all other beings as much as, or even more, than ourselves. I now know that this starts with forgiveness and acceptance of ourselves before others, and that unconditional love of all others cannot be achieved without self-forgiveness and love of our inner self.

CHAPTER 1

SWIRLING LIGHT

Cindy's voice:

I awoke at 5:30 am. Early for me, especially on a Saturday. I tried to go back to sleep. As I was reaching a sleep state, the word 'pen' popped into my head. It was strong and clear. I then remembered what Alec communicated, through the psychic medium, about writing early in the morning. I tried to go back to sleep, and there it was again—the word 'pen' in my head. Like it was imprinted on my brain.

I got up, leaving my husband Tom sleeping soundly, and went straight to the dining room table. It was dark, but I left the light off, so I would stay half asleep, thinking that I could be more receptive that way, in case Alec was going to help me write. Who knew if that was going to happen? I had never communicated directly with anyone in the afterlife, having only connected with Alec through three prior psychic medium sessions. I opened my journal and retrieved a pen from my desk, ready to start hand-writing any inspiration I received.

As I held my pen over the page, I started wondering, for the umpteenth time, what it was like for Alec when he got high. My pen started flowing. It wasn't like it was out of my control and writing words by itself. It wasn't being moved by another force. The words and emotions just popped into my mind, and I wrote them down as they flooded in. Sometimes I saw the words written, especially for the next topic area. Other times, entire sentences became my thoughts. The words flowed through my mind, to my hands, and onto the page.

Alec's voice:

Being high was nothingness. No racing thoughts, no pain, no isolation, just being there. No elation, no emotion. When did I get high? It was whenever. It was more recreational for me, even up to the day I woke up on the other side.

I woke up to such bright beauty and a bright light—like a train light, except it was swirling and with uneven edges. It wasn't moving toward or away from me, only swirling around, creating almost a tunnel effect. I was compelled to follow, though, to go into that light. It was the ultimate energy. So bright.

Cindy's voice:

At this point, Tom came into the room to ask if I was ok and if I wanted the light on. I quickly said, "NO!" I was worried I would lose my connection with Alec.

Immediately, words popped into my head: Be Kind.

Exactly like Alec.

Alec's voice:

I was submerged in feelings of total acceptance, that I could do, and have done, nothing wrong. I had the sense of being me, the true me, with no pretending to be someone else. Only me.

I wasn't flying, but I wasn't really floating either. Maybe drifting, like when I'd hang out in the ocean waves. I was suspended in the air. At least that was my initial perception. I moved by merely thinking myself there. My thought of the energy light ahead took me further toward it. Into what, I didn't know, but I wasn't scared. I was content. Rid of the feeling of not belonging. Rid of sadness and isolation.

I liked it. No. I loved it.

Love—I felt all-encompassing love surround me. Being loved, and me loving in return. I didn't love so much on my physical side. I loved you guys as my parents and family, but not many others. I was never 'in love' except maybe with my girlfriend in California. I loved Vera, as siblings do. The love I felt on the physical side was nothing like this.

The light was like a fire, but it wasn't burning. A constant, but gently swirling light with rough edges. Around the light was a different, darker color. Not black like the night, but a blue-gray that was comforting, and not scary. I wanted to go into the light. It wasn't calling or saying anything, but it drew me. It was a feeling that made me deeply yearn to go into it, as something I needed to do, to know, and to understand. Not in a mandatory way, but something I wanted more than anything to learn and understand—what it was, what was behind it, and why it was so bright. Brighter than anything I'd ever seen or even imagined.

I know people say there is a light in near-death experiences, and a tunnel. A tunnel is not quite what I saw. I can see why people might call it that, though. It was a hole in a huge space-time continuum that begged to be explored. I needed to see, to feel, and to sense what was there. What I was feeling was totally free. Free of all my harsh feelings from the physical side, and now full of nothing but positivity and love. Full and total acceptance of the true me; the inner me. The me I never fully knew myself, or let be seen by others. Even when high and my inhibitions left me, I was never this full of acceptance of myself or of others. This was much, much more than the nothingness and shedding of negativity, like being high. I was feeling so positive, so loved, and so fully accepted. I wanted to reach out to feel or sense what was around me. To explore it all and find out where I was. At one point, I thought *"Was I high?"* But I could tell, somehow, that it wasn't that at all. I was on the other side of physical life.

I paused. I wanted to go to you and Dad, because I was unsure where I was. I wanted to tell you where I was, and I thought of you and Dad. And then, you won't believe it, Mom, I was there. You were getting something out of the refrigerator in the garage. I could see you. Not as a physical presence, but more like a dream, with flashes of you and Dad. But I was there. I wasn't floating like a ghost, but I was all around you. You went upstairs, and Dad was taking one of his famous afternoon naps. I sensed immediately that you didn't know I was there. You were also unaware that I had died. I couldn't talk to you because you couldn't hear me.

I wondered again about the light, but then realized that I had never left it. It was there in front of me the whole time. Only a small part of me went to you and surrounded you.

Because I was everywhere, I was everything. I was connected to so many things. And I could 'tune into' things or places purely by thought. It was so cool!

I was drawn to what was before me, which brought me further in, and things changed as I 'moved' in. I can't say moved. It wasn't like there was space and time. I can't explain it. You become. Everything. All-encompassing. You are, and you just know.

My senses became increasingly hyperaware of my surroundings, yet calm, and full of acceptance and readiness to totally embrace what was to come. It wasn't scary. It's a beautiful experience to wrap all around you a blanket of full acceptance of who you truly are. Some say it's unconditional love. I suppose that's a good descriptor. I never really thought that much about unconditional love in my physical life.

What comes next? Who cares? It's not like you are anxious for the next second. There is no sense of seconds or minutes---only infinity. Plenty of time, or no time. The colors started to change as I was drawn in further. The surroundings changed. It was so beautiful. Colors I didn't know, never saw, and never even imagined. Shades of orange and blue and a white-yellow brightness not seen in the physical nature I knew. There were rocks along the way. A sort of trail… almost. I'm not good with words to describe this to you. It seemed to go on forever.

Cindy's voice:

I started to feel jittery and hyperventilate.

Alec's voice:

Calm down, Mom. I am a conduit. It's important to breathe. You can do this.

I became something different, absorbing all there is, and all there was. It wrapped all around me. I embraced it. I was, and it was. I was becoming –all—the wind, the stars, the mountains—everything. But not all at once. That would have been overwhelming. It was waves that came over me of perceptions and sensations, of being one with more and more. I didn't feel it physically because that was all gone. It was only in my consciousness.

It was enlightenment. I sensed I was on a higher level - a vibrational level. It was knowing, believing, being. I was there, but also everywhere. I went, and I saw. But I was never 'there' or 'here' or 'anywhere.' I was, and I knew. I was all around me and inside of me. I wasn't walking along a path, although it was clear where I was going. I just was.

I could think and be. It was all empowering. It was all-knowing. Yet I can't call it a feeling. It's more than that. More than one's physical sensing. It was the ultimate of *emotional being.*

Why can't you have this sort of love and acceptance on the physical side? It was meant to be and will be. Our souls love and reflect love. Love, and being, and acceptance.

No stress. Mom. You can do this.

"It's overwhelming me, Alec," I said shakily. "It's a lot to take in."

I know, but it is what it is, and it will be. Swallow and breathe. Love is all.

Find your true self. It's underneath all the fears you have. The doubts, the anxiety and worries—all the human feelings. There is an understanding here that when you doubt yourself, you doubt God, because He created you. Underneath all those doubts is your true self, and everyone has one. And that true self is beautiful. When you trust yourself, you trust the God in you.

In a way, you keep your personality here, but it becomes stronger, and so much more loving and accepting. Find your true self and you will understand.

I didn't feel it, Mom. I became it. Accepting. Loving. I hadn't encountered any others yet.

Look out the window at the beauty of the sunrise in the mountains where you are. Look at the soft edges and blurriness from the fog on top of the mountains. It's almost in pastel colors this early in the morning. There are so many parts of earth that I didn't see or appreciate in terms of their beauty. What a true pleasure it is to do that while on earth. It's a gift to be able to appreciate it while in your physical body.

It was my time to go when I did. I learned what had been intended for me to learn on that soul journey in my physical life on earth. And now I will begin my journey to become one with all. To know, to be, and to understand. And to become closer to the higher ones.

I must go. I have things to do, and you're exhausted. Loosen up. We'll have more conversations. How is Chico?

"He's good!" I declared. Chico was Alec's black cat with white paws that we inherited after his death. Having the cat around made us feel a little closer to Alec.

As the sun comes up, see the beauty, Mom. See the clouds, and the sun, and the mountains. I mean, really see them. And enjoy the beauty in all things. Yes, even spiders and webs. And art. Art is something that comes from people's physical mind and thoughts. Don't be overly influenced by what others may convey as heaven. Open your mind, and I will try to show you.

Cindy's voice:

I thought about what Alec had shared. The acceptance and peace he felt, and most of all, the abundance of love. Absorbing all of that, in a golden beautiful light, sounded like ultimate bliss.

At this point, in my mind, I saw what looked like an angel formed of light arching upward. Was it real? Was it my imagination? Then it was gone. And so was Alec. Our first transcendental writing was over. I was drained from the session and yet elated that I just finished a conversation with my deceased son.

CHAPTER 2

ABSORBING UNDERSTANDING

Cindy's voice:

On the second morning of writing, I slept a bit later. When I awoke, I went straight to the dining room table and picked up the pen. I held it to the page of the journal expectantly and hoped for a transcendental conversation with Alec again today.

I was still reeling from the conversation the day before. It was so hard to believe that my son was communicating with me about the afterlife. As I waited, I thought of the picturesque scenes that Alec described of his immediate experience following his passing. It was beautiful. Not only in the views that he shared, but also in the abundant love and acceptance, and the intense light. It gave me hope.

Alec's voice:

The tunnel that everyone talks about is not really a tunnel. There is a light at the end, though, drawing you into it, but you can't see the sides. They appear to be the edges of the light. It was a hill-like structure, with rocks in a unique color of yellow from the light that shines. Not a color of rock that you see on earth. Every soul sees something different but pleasing to them. The light doesn't reach you. It draws you in because you are so focused on its brightness. You see or notice little else.

It's not a path, but it's like a path. You see and know the way. You want to go in toward the light. You know you don't have to, and it's not scary. It feels like a choice, but one that is extremely easy to make.

I sensed myself as the 'me' that I never knew. I was no longer the physical me, but the essence of me. I knew I had died, but I didn't remember dying, nor the specifics of my dying.

My essence, or spirit, was sensing more and more of the whole vastness of the universe. I'm glad it was only a little at a time. Having it all at once would have overwhelmed my essence–my soul.

I knew things. I was becoming 'in tune' with things in the physical world I had not appreciated in my life. The wind, the sun, the mountains, the grass, the trees. Again, everything was connected to me, and I to them. I knew when the wind was about to blow and where, or that the rain was coming in a certain area, but not elsewhere. I simply knew these things. It was not difficult, like in my physical body, when my mind raced because of my ADHD (Attention Deficit Hyperactivity Disorder). On the contrary, it was peaceful, merely knowing that I knew these things.

There was no sense of time. I don't know how long I was on that path, absorbing and knowing.

My essence was weightless. I was an illuminated orb that sometimes became more humanoid shaped. I was a ball of energy that was reflected as light. Energy, love, and being.

I learned a lot along that 'path' as I absorbed and became the knowing essence of me. Along that path, there was a download of knowledge into my essence and understanding.

I always loved learning, even though my school grades didn't show it. The learning part, without the homework and tests, was fun. Well, not so much history, English, and languages, but I loved the science, math, and, of course, technology. Now I was absorbing so much knowledge about science and math–how things are and always were connected---and how they worked. It was amazing. Enlightening. So much knowledge that is not actually known by our physical selves. Physical humans have so much to learn. Spirits in this realm have an incredible amount of knowledge and experience.

As I was going in toward the light, I saw small lights shaped like orbs in the distance. As they got closer, I could see that they were shaped like an oblong orb, slowly drawing toward me. I wasn't scared. All I sensed was acceptance, welcoming, and love.

A wave of recognition swept over me, and I was happy to see other essences, or souls, that I knew. Papa, your father, was the first one. Mom-Mom was next, with a grandfather I knew was Pop-Pop, but had not known during my physical life. All my extended relatives, some of whom I had met but paid little attention to, were there to greet me. You had such a big family, Mom. Others I had never met, but somehow also knew who they were. Mama Mac and Pop (your grandparents) welcomed me, too, and I could sense Nana and others, including you, Mom, in their essence.

The Russian ancestors of my birth parents were there, too. I knew none of them in my physical life, but somehow, I knew immediately who they were.

I have many ancestral families, and each of my ancestors has a huge number of ancestral families. But somehow, it's not overwhelming. All of them surrounded me with love and total acceptance, to welcome me when I arrived. Even my birthmother's ancestors did that, although she had offered me up for adoption when I was an infant. I now know it was out of love. I can't tell you what it was like to have all of them surround me, welcoming me, and enveloping me in love and acceptance.

It's funny because I never completely accepted myself when I was physically living. I was different from everyone else. I was always trying to be what society wanted me to be, or whatever I thought society wanted of me. I never really understood I could simply be me. The closest I ever was to being me was when I was around you and Dad.

But now I could sense and be the true me, and every soul totally accepted me. They didn't want me to be anyone else. It was a wonderful feeling that filled my essence with pure bliss. Pure acceptance. Pure love. Unconditional love in its purist form.

All my ancestors and relatives surrounded me and embraced me in light. I welcomed it, even though on the physical side, I didn't like hugs. There is no time and no place, so I don't know how long I was there with them surrounding me. I was totally safe, protected, and accepted in love.

The swirling light was still there but didn't have the same pull as before. It was simply there in the background while I was embraced. As if it were waiting for me.

It was so freeing to relax and settle into being the true me. Me, with none of the struggles of isolation and depression, and my Asperger's characteristics. Only the inner me. No physical constraints, no worry about acne, or teeth, or my weight. Only the inner me.

I was bathed in light from the energies of the hundreds of souls of my ancestors. The energy made me feel powerful. Like I could, and should, do anything I wanted. But mainly, I wanted to get to know my true self. It was clear that I didn't know my inner me, and

I could sense that this was something important that I needed to understand. Self-love would be my first focus.

The acceptance and love I sensed seemed to eliminate any fear of trying to understand who I truly was. That's not the way it was for me on the physical side. I was never in tune with who I was, or what I felt.

Mom, I think you are scared sometimes to look at your inner self and understand the true you. Try to let go of those fears. Unfortunately, every little doubt and fear disrupts the waves of trust in yourself and in God. It's important on your journey to get to know your true inner self. You will do that only through peace and quiet, and by relaxation. It is only in this quiet that you can hear the guidance from the spiritual realm. You have such a short time on earth in your physical body.

As I was embraced, the understanding of the true me was already underway. I was absorbing the true me while simultaneously absorbing the energy of all my ancestors and loved ones.

I realized I had so much to learn about myself, my past physical life, and about the universes and, well, about everything. I was looking forward to that, but not forward in time. There is no time. Only stages or levels, dimensions, you might call them. We pass through stages of learning. I didn't know it, but I was about to embark on an eternity of learning. It's so cool!

My loved ones showed me what the afterlife was like, and its incredible beauty. We have our own realm. We are aware of yours on the physical side, but on the spirit side, we have our own realm of splendor. There are beautiful hills, rocks, lakes, and sky. The colors are indescribable—more vivid, bright, vibrant, and full of an energy that simply can't be imagined.

After I was greeted by my loved ones and relatives, they accompanied me into a vastness that can't be described. The enormity and boundlessness of it was almost overwhelming. They gradually brought me toward a light that seemed to be contained in a pseudo-spherical shape, and I knew I was supposed to go into it. When I did, I was bathed in a light that was warm, enriching, cleansing, and healing. It made me feel whole again, and I started remembering that I was here before. It eased the pain and struggles that my soul had dealt with in my physical life. While it didn't wash them away, it made the pain almost go away, so I could look at it more objectively. I can't describe how wonderful it made me feel. Virtuous, loved, and healed from all the ravages of my self-destructive, prior physical life.

My spirit guide is, and was, always with me. In my physical life and spiritual one. She has a strong love and sense of caring for my soul, and she ensures that I have the best experience I can, always. We reviewed my physical experience on earth in this past life, and what I was able to learn. Not in a critical way, but rather in a way that helped us understand how my choices came about, and their impact on my life and other beings. There were video sequences to review of your life experience. This is why people say their life flashes by them right before they die. You are always your own worst critic. Many of the choices that I made weren't recognized by me as *choices* at the time. Many times, I could have made better decisions. My spirit guide helped me see that those were learning opportunities, and my choices were what made the learning real and helped me grow and understand.

Our experience in the physical world is intended to teach us how our choices and decisions either guide us toward, or away from, a more loving soul. That means loving ourselves first. I was very critical of myself. I had flaws and mental health illnesses in my physical life that embarrassed me, even though I acted like they didn't. I was always trying to hide my quirks merely to fit in, but I really should have simply been me, quirks and all. In evaluating my physical experience, I looked at how each choice led to either the deterioration of relationships or the building of them. I'm afraid many of my decisions were self-destructive.

In the spiritual realm, we are always introspective, trying to understand, and learn, and grow spiritually. We strive to love all beings, to be basked in love for ourselves and for all others, even those that have wronged us, or been terribly evil.

We are meant to maximally learn from the choices we made in the physical life, and we strive for a balance across our many prior, and future, physical lives. Yes, a soul can have many experiences of physical life. If we experienced a series of physical lives that were hard and involved a lot of struggles, we might have a lighter, happier one in our next physical life to balance things out. The reason for the evaluation of the learnings is to understand the intention and learning that came from the choices we made. We aren't judged for our choices, but we look at whether the choices helped us learn what was intended. Conscience is the soul's responsibility. Our soul must learn from decisions and choices that we make in our incarnations. It is all about growing and learning, allowing us to understand and to love all others and ourselves.

After reviewing learnings from my physical life with my spirit guide, there are higher guides that review and evaluate the learnings from the physical life experience. This is intended to review the key learnings from this physical life, and whether it was sufficient for the intention. Sometimes we are not able to live the physical life and have the learnings that we are meant to have. I was supposed to learn about the seduction and struggles of substance use disorders and addiction, and I did learn that. I also learned about living with mild mental health illnesses. The higher spirit guides look across the prior physical lives of my soul to understand what experiences are still needed.

The evaluation of the learnings never ends. We are constantly reviewing our past lives, the learnings from them, and what other learnings we need for our divine soul to grow and come closer to the higher beings, and God.

I know now that there really does exist a divine higher being that I call God. I also know there will be many levels of learning before I get close to an inkling of the understanding that would allow me to grasp the enormity and vastness, the all-encompassing nature, of that Higher Being. God is so inconceivable in the vastness of energy, connectedness, and understanding of All Things that exist, as the creator of All Things. God knows no evil and could create no evil. He only knows all-encompassing love. It is impossible to absorb and appreciate that without learning. And so we have extensive learning.

All my loved ones accepted me for my true, inquisitive self. They somehow knew that my intelligence was never fully realized on the physical side, trapped as it was by the mental health conditions and addiction tendencies.

My ancestors and I stayed on that path to the intense beautiful light for what seemed like a long time, but it could have been seconds, or millions of years. One time, I wondered if we were blocking the path for others, but was immediately reassured by my ancestors, collectively, that every soul has a different path to follow. When I say communicate, it was by thought. Whatever they thought came into my knowing. Communication is completely by thought and emotion in the spiritual realm.

Oh, and Lexi (our maltipoo dog) and Bucky (our cockapoo dog) are here too. It was wonderful to sense their loving loyalty to me, like they were in my physical lifetime.

Let's continue tomorrow. But earlier, Mom!

Cindy's voice:

It was clear our session was ending, and at that point, a picture came into my mind. Brown-yellow and lavender hills on either side of an energy path to a large light swirl, with smaller yellow rocks to the sides of the energy path. A central orb surrounded by hundreds of energy orbs embracing it, with total acceptance and love conveyed through the softness of the colors and lines. The sky of early dawn, with light on the horizon in off-white, moving up into dull blue and rising to a night sky.

Our second transcendental conversation was complete. He shared so much with me. The descriptions of how he met with family and ancestors and how he felt made me smile. I always told him that family and love are everything! It was hard to imagine how he connected with everything. Maybe it was merely something that mortal beings can't grasp. It was also hard for me to imagine reviewing every choice I'd made in my physical life, even in fast-forward mode. Alec made it sound so easy. Of course, he always made things sound easy when he was alive, too. Alec was incredibly bright in his physical life. I couldn't wait to find out what else he would reveal.

CHAPTER 3

REMEMBERING

Cindy's voice:

Memories of Alec flooded my consciousness. I remembered seeing Alec for the first time in the orphanage outside of Kaliningrad, Russia. His face was full of anticipation and curiosity, looking all around him and wondering who Tom and I were, and what life had in store for him. We were ecstatic to be able to adopt this sweet, beautiful boy.

As a toddler, Alec had blonde hair and hazel eyes which made him look almost angelic. He was the happiest kid growing up. His smile could light up a room, and his laugh was incredibly contagious. He had a great sense of humor, and could make you laugh, even when you weren't in the mood. You always knew when he was truly excited, because he would literally jump up and down and shake his hands in a display of true, unfiltered joy. Even as he got older, there was never any doubt when he was excited. Whether about chocolate cake or ice cream, or burgers, fries, and Coca-Cola. He would get especially excited about a new piece of technology or video game. A window seat on a long flight, or landing a plane himself in a flight simulator, also excited him, as did his cat, Chico. His expressions of excitement and joy are some of the many things that we miss so much about him.

When Alec became interested in something, he would immerse himself in it. Early on, it was the weather, and as a toddler, the weather channel was his absolute favorite. As he grew older, it became electricity, and then technology. Like most people of his generation, he liked video gaming, but his true passion was computer programming (or coding, as it's called now), and it eventually became his superpower. In early middle school, he was consuming college-level programming manuals cover to cover, and simply couldn't get enough. He saved money to buy computer components to build his own souped-up machine, complete with liquid-filled coolers to handle the heat created by the speed and processing loads. He was a very bright and talented young man.

Alec had high-functioning autism (formerly called Asperger's syndrome, which Alec preferred, so that term is used in the telling of his story), combined with attention-deficit hyperactivity disorder (ADHD). He was somewhat awkward socially, and tended to be somewhat of a loner who needed his own time and space, yet he could talk for hours about his strong interests and passions. In educational testing, he was off the charts in math, but low in reading comprehension. This meant that his interests and strengths gravitated almost solely toward science and technology.

He was always excited to share some new technology or software with us. We, and many of our family and friends, used him as an in-home "Help Desk," because he could solve almost any technology issue. Alec loved to help others and teach about technology, and he was a patient and thoughtful instructor. We were incredibly proud of him.

CHAPTER 4

LIGHT AND LEARNING

Cindy's voice:

I asked the divine self and spirit guides of Alec, and my own divine self (soul) to speak through me: to show me, and share with me, what should be shared with the physical side. I specifically asked this morning because I was distracted by what the day held already, and workers were arriving to start our kitchen demolition for a remodel. I was anxious to learn what Alec might share with me today. His first descriptions of what he experienced as he entered the afterlife were beautiful and fascinating. Alec responded, and I did the best I could to capture everything amid the distractions.

Alec's voice:

The path that I was on toward the light got brighter and brighter, to the extent that the light was becoming part of me. My arms were absorbing the light and becoming seemingly longer, like there were light extensions to my hands. Maybe this was because the light had no definite lines, and the fuzzy edges seemed to extend to all parts of my body. I was becoming one with the light. The more I progressed into the light, and the more I learned as a soul, the more that light became part of my essence.

But at some point, I arched upward, almost as if my essence couldn't take more light. At least not yet. I wasn't ready.

As I veered upward, I felt so incredibly free to go in any direction—an infinite number of directions—to explore the universe and beyond. And I wanted to explore it all. To learn, to understand. Yet I knew at least some of what was there. Even though I never 'learned it,' I just knew.

Knowledge was a thought away and was building substantially in me. If someone on the physical side had only a fraction of the knowledge I now know, they would scare mankind, or be thought insane! The knowledge that was building in me wasn't history, although the history of the universe and how it formed was part of it. I was highly focused on the way things were all connected. The stars, the moons, the planets, and the galaxies beyond our solar system. I was no longer bound to earth and its rotation around the sun. I was way beyond that and starting to understand other planetary systems and universes.

It is so beautiful, Mom. All that God created, and then the course of events that took place to form all that is. Simply beautiful.

I loved being among the stars and planets, but it seemed that there was something I needed to do. It wasn't urgent. I could take my 'time,' but I sensed that there was another stage after this exploration that I was doing. I accepted this without question. I knew I needed to follow the light. The light that was larger and brighter than all the others.

There were an infinite number of 'paths' that I could follow, but my ancestors were still with me, guiding me to a specific one. It was a beautiful path and one that was filled with light and vivid colors. Maybe that's why my ancestors chose it for me. It seemed like it was meant for me.

There were grassy mountains in less vibrant colors. Some were muted purple, and some of the rocks were yellow. The sky was a vibrant blue, unlike any sky color I'd ever seen, but blue, nonetheless. There was water, too. A stream with rocks that created a bubbling noise. Is 'babbling brook' the expression?

In the background, I could hear music. You know I never liked music with vocals, but this music had little vocalization. It was mainly a single, very calming, peaceful tone, sometimes two tones, and occasionally, a brief, pretty melody would break out on piano or flute. I know the medium told you I was very musical but didn't pursue it. I think a piano teacher once told me I had perfect pitch. But piano wasn't for me. I eventually liked electronic synthesizer music, or techno music, with the steady beat that I used a lot for studying. It calmed me. Maybe because it was a fast, steady beat in tune with my brain waves or something.

There were clouds swirling in white, and sometimes in different bright colors, but I always knew they were clouds that were colored. Or at least I thought they were. It's possible they were different paths for different souls–I really don't know. Maybe I'll learn someday.

It came into my consciousness what I needed to do. It's strange how I become aware of something because it comes into my thoughts. That's how we communicate with each other here too, by thinking and emotion. And it conveys to others what we are trying to communicate. There is no need to learn foreign languages here.

What I needed to do was not explore the universes, although that's important, too. First, I needed self-exploration, reflection, and introspection. I needed to understand and know my true inner self before I could go to the next stage. I never spent much time on that while on the physical side.

They say your whole life flashes by when you are about to die. Mine didn't do that. I merely woke up on the other side. But it did flash by peripherally while I was on this side. You see, there are multiple tracks playing in my consciousness simultaneously. So many I can't count them. Yet I can follow an almost infinite number of them. I knew there would be more to learn about my past physical life and how it shaped me. It was time to learn, truly learn about who I was, who I am, and how I was shaped by experiences in this life, as well as past lives. It was time to understand my true self identity and what it means.

My spirit guide, who is part of my divine soul, edged me to a 'place' where there were many souls; not only my ancestors. There were different levels where one could learn, and souls were spread across them. I was eager to learn. About everything. How things work and are connected. How souls exist as energy, and how they communicate and grow. I was excited and happy to be able to learn. I gravitated to a level that was right for me, and for what I needed to learn.

Before I started learning about my true inner self, it seemed I needed to learn a little about how everything is connected.

I reviewed God's plan and how creation took place once again, plus all the subsequent events that shaped mountains and combined or split seas. It wasn't "book learning." It was like watching a movie with no sound or narration. I watched and absorbed so much in a short time. This was also a review since I had been introduced to this during my prior time in the spiritual realm. If only learning could take place like this on the physical side!

You're distracted today, Mom.

"I know. Too much is going on. The dog and cat, and Dad moving things around. Workers coming."

Try to focus. I may not be able to come through for these conversations for very long.

There was more structure in the learning center than I'd seen before. I could learn and learn, and then join my family when I wanted. I learned a lot about my family too—your family, Dad's family, and that of my birthmother and father.

The stages, or levels, of learning were circular so that you could learn a great deal of introductory-level material about a topic and then, if you wanted, you could continue that topic and gain even deeper knowledge. It was like layered circles, within layered circles, within layered circles. Remember those mazes that Vera and I used to do with crayons when we went to restaurants? Some were square and some were rounded, and you started at one point and tried to get to the 'end' without hitting a dead-end? Think of the round ones, with layer upon layer of circles. That's the best way I can explain the learning circle. Like a round maze that is infinite, and each layer is a topic that goes on forever to the level you want to learn. Your medium likened it to mirrors, within mirrors, within mirrors. The mirror visual metaphor was intended to depict looking at your true self.

Even though the circles continued infinitely, I could pause and go see my ancestors and loved ones whenever I wanted, which I did often. Papa and I hang out together. We're best pals. He is learning too, and we learn from each other, although he's always saying he learns so much more from me. When I say my ancestors and loved ones are always around, I mean it, because I am connected to them. But they also belong to different families and soul groups. So do I. You can be part of many, many family/ancestral groups and other soul groups simultaneously. It's amazing. I was never good at multi-tasking, but this is the ultimate in it, and it's effortless.

It was time to learn about my true inner self. There was going to be a lot of introspection and truth. I have lived many lives. My soul is made up of all those experiences. When a new experience is needed, a part of my divine self is born into a physical body to gain that experience, while most of my soul remains in the afterlife.

We each have a divine true self that is our soul, and it has been that way throughout the history of mankind. In the afterlife, we are constantly helping one another. All out of love. All our thoughts are transparent; there are no secrets from one another.

You can appeal to the spirit guides of your divine soul to help you and guide you in your physical life. In particular, the spirit guides and teacher spirits of your divine soul, and your guardian angel, can help you with the decisions and struggles you face. Your guardian angel and life guides are assigned to you at birth, and stay with you, specifically to help you achieve your life purpose. These high vibrational beings offer pure unconditional love and can impart knowledge and wisdom to you when needed. Teacher guides are wise and practical and can help guide you along your path, especially when you wander off. Then there are other guides, like creative guides, that help you open up your imagination and creativity. Joy guides that encourage you to find hobbies that bring you joy, healing guides to help you during stressful times and connect you with your physical, emotional, mental, and spiritual health. There are so many.

I never knew about all these spirit guides. Most people don't.

Cindy's voice:

I certainly hadn't known to appeal to the spirit guides and teacher spirits of my divine soul, though I had heard of guardian angels. I didn't realize that I could appeal to them throughout my life. This was enlightening. I especially wondered about my guardian angel and life guides. How do I reach them? I thought the learning sessions sounded incredible. What a great resource! I also wondered if you ever got caught in that learning maze and got lost!

Towards the end of this session, Alec revealed he lived prior lives. This intrigued me, as I never really believed in reincarnation, thinking it was only the creation of somebody's imaginative mind. Reincarnation was something I'd heard about my entire life, but never knew much about. I was determined to keep an open mind. These transcendental conversations with Alec were fascinating, and I couldn't wait for the next day.

CHAPTER 5

LEARNING AND TEACHING

Cindy's voice:

Another foggy, rainy day on the physical side. I'm anxious to hear more about the learning resources and the teaching that Alec does. Hopefully, he will share more details about all of that with me today. As I waited, I pondered what Alec shared in our last session about spirit guides and his prior lives. I wondered if he would share more about both topics at some point. I waited, thinking how fortunate I was to be communicating with him, and how much hope it gave me.

Alec's voice:

It's so beautiful in the afterlife. Sometimes I pause in my intensive learning and bask in the beauty outside of the learning levels. Whatever you think is beautiful is here, and you can think your way to it. If you think about mountains, you will be among them. The same with the ocean or plains.

My focus initially was on learning about how everything is connected. Family, yes, but mostly about how important it is to understand your true self.

What was mine is no longer mine. And who I am is not exactly mine either. It's hard to explain, but I'll try.

We are created as physical beings because our divine soul needs a certain experience. Our divine self can look at what will happen during a lifetime before a baby is conceived and decide if it's the right learning experience for them.

It is our divine soul that decides if an experience is needed for learning and growth, and they create a new physical being to have that experience. A tiny part of the divine soul's essence is born physically as a baby and will live out that lifetime of experience to learn and grow the divine soul. The whole reason for life is to understand and build compassion and forgiveness. That same acceptance and love that bathes over us after we die, when our loved ones welcome us to the afterlife.

Don't be sad, Mom. I see your tears. I sense your sadness. Yes, my physical life experience was known to my divine self before I was born, and you and Dad were meant to adopt me. My life played out exactly as it should have and was expected to.

I'm learning how to be introspective. I never learned that on the physical side. But I need to be able to understand and learn my inner self before I can advance to another stage. I needed a reminder of how to be introspective from my prior time in the spiritual world.

Mom, if you start thinking of life as something to experience and learn from, and not something that is happening to you, it will help you let go of a lot of your fears and anxiety. You cannot control that much of your life, and it will happen as it is supposed to. You have some choices to make but otherwise, it will play out as it was written. It's like one of those movies where the audience can choose the direction the story goes at a few points in the show. Only there are many more choices you make along the way. Even the bad times are a lesson and experience that you need to have. So, experience life. Grab it. Make as much of it as you can.

"Alec, when people die, why don't they become one with their divine soul again immediately?"

Great question, Mom. Becoming one again with your divine soul is earned after you get the most learning out of your recent physical experience. You need to review the physical life experience that you were meant to have in your physical life, and understand why you needed it, compared to your actual experience, and what you learned. This will help you get the most learning out of the experience. It is important to complete the evaluation of the learnings in your prior physical life, so that your soul and higher spirit guides can decide whether the intended learnings occurred, or whether you need another experience to learn what was truly intended.

"Do you know how my life is going to play out, Alec? Can you see it, or can only my divine self?"

I can see parts of it … like flashes.

Papa and I sometimes hang out together and marvel at the beauty of it here. We also talk about how freeing it is to be rid of all our worries, physical pain, and struggles–like Papa's dementia and heart problems. Or like my ADHD and Asperger's. It really is so freeing not to be bound and constrained by a physical body. Then inevitably we end up talking about the science of connectedness, the vastness of the universe, and the enormity and power of our inner self.

Our inner self is made up of feelings and emotions, beliefs, and judgement, and yes, even views of politics. We need to examine every fragment of those, and it is hard work. But the great thing about me is I did it quickly, more so than most. Because I avoided conflict and emotions on the physical side, I didn't have as much to understand from this past physical life as many others.

My journey from death to exploring, to learning about connectedness, to my introspective learning, has also been relatively quick, even though I have no sense of time. I only know that because I'm further along than other souls who died before me. Now I can take my time and explore while I'm learning. I can also be with you in these transcendental conversations! I may not always be able to do that once I advance to other stages.

Aside from learning, we have tasks to do for the greater good of all, and every soul has a function. We exist only for love, kindness to others, and beauty. And we all work with a joyful attitude, which doesn't often happen with physical humans in their work. We have activities like concerts, and the most beautiful poetry and art. I like the music here, although I would have scoffed at it on the physical side. There is background music playing all the time. It helps me learn. But concerts are more intense in melody and drama.

My next step on the journey was to review my life. It is part of understanding and becoming the true me. I reviewed my entire lifetime and where I made each major choice. I can see how each choice played out, and I can choose different choices and see what would have happened. It's all part of the learning and evaluation of the physical life experience.

We don't have food here. But sometimes we think of food and how much we enjoyed certain things to eat on the physical side. Like cheeseburgers! Chocolate ice cream! But I don't crave it. Our sustenance here is love, compassion, understanding, truth, and acceptance of all others and All Things. And there is the feeling of ultimate satisfaction when you embrace all of that.

Mom, you should try to learn more about meditation and self-awakening. It would help you understand who you really are. It is the next phase of your life. You had a successful career. Soon, you should let the business go and focus on you.

"You have a lot of wisdom for me today, Alec."

Yeah Mom. I've learned a lot.

"How do you teach, Alec? Do you make the 'movies' through thought that play out for other souls to learn?"

Yes, I send those thoughts as the learning.

So much here that is beautiful. So many dimensions to experience, so many realms to understand.

I will be here when you arrive, Mom. Waiting for you, to show you everything. So will Papa and all your family.

"Will you be there for Nana, Alec?"

Yes, Papa and I will be waiting right there. So will her mother and father, and all her siblings. Even her grandmother, the one she called Mama, that she used to take care of when she was little.

This is a continuation of physical life. Although not in our physical bodies, we remember everything that happened in our lifetime—even things we weren't quite in tune with—like choices we made that we didn't realize were choices. And we learn so much about our lifetime. There is no judgement if we made bad choices. Again, it's like watching a movie. When you watch a movie, you don't feel regretful or guilty about all the choices made in the plot, although you might feel disappointment that they made a choice you wouldn't have made. That's simply part of compassion.

I do not feel regret for what I did and the choices I made in my lifetime. I do wish that I could have done that without hurting you and Dad, as I said earlier. The choice to use drugs was bad, but it was what I was supposed to learn and experience. So now I can view my life as the experience it was meant to be. The day I died, I didn't realize that Kratom would be toxic, and I didn't know that I could overdose on it. I ordered it online, not even on the dark web. But it was my time to die. I lived long enough to gain the experience I needed to learn. My life was designed and envisioned by my divine soul to be a short learning experience. I was needed in the afterlife to help other souls learn. It's amazing how everything is connected and depends on everything and everyone else.

"Is the learning cycle like circles that never end, within circles that never end, within circles?"

Yes. Learning never stops. I've heard you say that the day you stop learning is the day you stagnate and don't want to work anymore. You don't have to worry about that here. I told you that in your last medium session. Learning is infinite. And as things change, the learning changes.

"What about the old souls from way, way back? Do they keep learning?"

Yes, they do, but they have probably already learned their true inner self through review of all their prior lives of experience and learning and reached more purity of love. They may not have physical incarnations anymore. They are themselves, but also one with their divine self as well. Yet the elders, as we call them, can still learn.

Our divine self is made up of many, many incarnations of prior lives. We become one with our divine self when we have truly learned all there is to know about ourselves and our life choices and experiences.

"Alec, what about other spiritual beings like our guardian angel? Is it true we each have one? Is there more than one? What about spiritual guides?"

Yes, beings on the physical side have a guardian angel, who is a part of our divine self and assigned to watch over the human as they experience their reincarnated life. Each physical life as a mortal has a spirit guide and teacher spirits that they can ask for help and direction. Dad should ask for help when he gets lost and won't ask for driving directions!

You can appeal to the spirit guides of your higher self for guidance and help. Your divine self is watching over all the incarnations that are in physical learning experiences, and there are an almost infinite number of them. All your spiritual guides and spirit teachers are part of your higher self. They are the ones that act on behalf of your divine self.

All divine souls are part of God's creation and become one with God once all the experiences of that soul are gained. But that is very rare. Only Jesus has achieved that. Jesus IS God. He became one with God, but still watches over all of us.

"Alec, why do all three mediums mention Joshua?"

Because it is who I aspire to be. Joshua is an older Hebrew spelling and pronunciation for Jesus. We can feel God's energy. It is so all-encompassing, it's impossible to be in His presence without becoming pure, and that requires a great deal of learning. The energy is so intense and the light so bright. We all aspire to be one with God, but we must become pure first.

Center yourself, Mom. You're getting anxious about what you need to do today for work.

"I know. It's part of being human."

Yes, I suppose, but you could relax more. Let go of all those anxieties.

Love is all. Be kind. Be your best self. It all works out in the end.

Cindy's voice:

Alec gave me lots of sound advice this session. The journey to understand your true self must be fascinating. Alec always found introspection and reflection difficult. So had I. Maybe he will have some tips for me.

CHAPTER 6

CHECKING THINGS OUT

Tom's voice:

When your twenty-one-year-old son is not answering texts or phone calls for days, it puts you in a tailspin of angst, and invokes worry bordering on panic. Couple this with the head of Human Resources at our son's employer calling me to share that Alec was underperforming, and looking 'pretty rough,' and you must go check things out for yourself. Alec was an intern with this artificial intelligence (AI) software company, and converted to full-time employment two months earlier. The head of Human Resources said, "If I were his father, I would want to know." That prompted a trip to Washington, D.C. to check on him a few days later. Not fully thinking things through, I left a message that I was coming the day before, and by the time I arrived, everything seemed fine. After I left, he went right back to not responding to texts and messages.

A continued pattern of sparse communication, and two weeks later, I again traveled to D.C. This time, I didn't tell Alec I was coming. We thought it might be better to check on him unannounced. At Cindy's prompting, I even turned off the family tracking app we had been using since high school.

I started the six-hour drive to Washington, D.C. early in the morning. I worried the whole way about what I might find. Alec was still at work when I arrived mid-afternoon. I managed to get into the lobby of his apartment building when someone left the building and waited for him to get home. I was anxious. It was getting late. I wondered if he had just been busy or had met friends to hang out with after work. He might have even lost his phone and not had time to replace it. None of these alternative reasons kept my worries at bay. Previous experiences caused worry to continue clouding my mind.

Several people came and went over the next couple of hours, but finally, he came in through the lobby doors. He was shocked to see me sitting there. Alec was unkempt, and it looked like he hadn't combed his hair in a while. Classic Alec, this wasn't too unusual.

"Dad, what are you doing here?"

"I came to see you. To check if you're okay. You haven't been answering our calls or texts again."

Alec didn't respond.

"Let's go upstairs," I said, jerking my head toward the elevator and standing up.

He hesitated. "Don't you want to go out to dinner or something?"

I said, "No, it's too early for that. Let's go upstairs and talk. Then we can go out and grab something to eat."

He seemed defeated. I started toward the elevator, and he followed uncertainly. The elevator in that old building is unbelievably slow. Alec gnawed on his nails, an old nervous habit.

I tried to sound casual. "How was work, bud? Everything going OK?"

"Good", he mumbled. He was distracted, and his eyes darted around. He continued picking at his fingernails, a sure sign of his anxiety.

Alec never really talked a whole lot socially, or with the family. At least not unless it was a topic he was really interested in, like technology. Then, he would talk your ears off.

Alec was not in a chatty mood today. Distant, and in his own world, I wondered what he was thinking. Maybe his mind was still at work? Or he just didn't know what to say?

Alec had been lonely living by himself in a city where he knew no one. He wasn't very social, even with co-workers, but he had started exploring the city by electric scooter and metro, and he seemed happy when we did get a chance to speak with him. At first, that was usually once a week, but more recently, the communication was very sporadic.

Alec's apartment was tiny, about two hundred-twenty-five square feet with a modest closet, a kitchenette area and small bath. Anyone could get claustrophobic in that studio apartment, I thought, as we walked to his apartment door.

Alec fumbled with the keys. He tried to say the key didn't always work. I took the keys and opened the door.

The odor hit me first. I looked around. Every surface covered. My heart dropped into my stomach. I thought I was going to be sick. I stood there in disbelief. I couldn't even think straight.

Drugs and drug paraphernalia covered every surface. Alec was never very good at cleaning his room at home, but this was a whole new level of mess. It was a train wreck. But what was most devastating was that there were so. many. drugs. Multiple vape pens and torch lighters. Cannisters that stunk like skunk littered his desk that doubled as his table. Odd-shaped pieces of something bluish and shiny that I would learn were crystal meth, and all kinds of pills were strewn all over. Rolled up dollar bills and empty pen cartridges lay next to powder mounds on paper. Alec said nothing. Not a word. He moved to start cleaning things up, but I stopped him.

"Don't touch anything," I said.

I looked around the kitchenette and found a large trash bag and just started tossing. It took over an hour to get it all bagged and wipe the desk and floor clean. Then I started searching.

"This would be a whole lot easier if you just told me where the rest is hidden, son," I said.

"This is all of it," he claimed.

I found more paraphernalia in his dresser drawers and closet. And a lot of pot in his bookbag. I was thinking to myself, 'I hope he doesn't take that to work'. Then it hit me. Work? Work doesn't matter. This was much bigger than work. This is a major problem.

Standing in the hallway just outside the apartment, I called Cindy and updated her. She was just as distraught as I was. We waited an hour to discuss what to do because we needed time for things to sink in, and to think more clearly about what to do next. We were totally unprepared for the magnitude of this. We both agreed something drastic had to be done.

After hanging up with Cindy, Alec and I had an awkward talk. I tried to stay calm, but my insides were screaming. I felt devastated that Alec had chosen this path. To think that all his amazing potential could be lost to substance abuse. I was living a parent's nightmare. We knew he needed help, but also that he needed to want to be helped. I asked him if he was willing to get into a program and get some help. I explained things couldn't go on this way. That he would lose his job, and possibly even his life. He told me he was getting his drugs on the dark web. I tried to help him understand how easy it could be to get a bad batch of any one of the substances he was experimenting with, and that could be the end. He agreed to getting into a program.

I told Alec I wanted him to move into the hotel with me for the next few days. He was in no shape to go to work the next day, and he slept most of it. Detox started the following night, and he had a seizure in the early hours of the morning. I felt helpless, and this only reinforced how bad things were. Not only was he using, but he was strung out.

I identified an outpatient program for Alcoholics Anonymous (AA) / Narcotics Anonymous (NA), which he started the very next day. He needed evening meetings so he could continue to work. Three evenings a week, plus a meeting on the weekend, was how he started.

With good attendance, the frequency of meetings would taper off until it was once a week after thirty days. They did random drug tests and held people accountable. It sounded like a reasonable program. I accompanied him to his first evening meeting and met the leader that night.

We moved to an AirBnB for the next week. I didn't feel comfortable leaving him in such a vulnerable state, and wanted to be sure he got enough meetings under his belt to hopefully begin to make a difference. This also allowed me to thoroughly clean out his apartment before he moved back in. Two weeks after starting the outpatient program, I found Alec a sober coach in D.C. that could call him frequently, and meet with him in person at least weekly. I knew my wife and I couldn't stay in D.C. long-term. This just might work, I thought to myself.

Alec and the coach talked by phone and seemed to get along, so they met for coffee the following Saturday. We walked to the coffee meeting, but after the initial introductions, I left and waited in a nearby park. He had to do this himself. And it was the rules of the sober coach network, anyway. Alec needed to ask for help himself, and to openly admit he had a problem, if he was going to have a chance at real recovery.

Having established a local support system for Alec, it was time to head back home. Obviously, I was still worried. After seeing how deeply involved he was with the various drugs, I was sure there would never be another time that I would not worry.

At least he was in an outpatient program with random testing, talking with people who understood substance abuse, and meeting regularly with a sober coach. Cindy and I had a plan, and were, at least, ahead of where we had been a short few weeks ago.

CHAPTER 7

INFINITE DIMENSIONS

Cindy's voice:

I t is later in the day, as the morning got away from me. The clouds over the mountains have a soft touch, making the peaks of the mountains blue, topped with white clouds. God created such beauty on the physical side, too. I pray to my divine soul, my spirit guide and teacher spirits, and to my guardian angel, to guide me and give me direction in writing–this time typing directly on the page instead of writing in the journal.

I was having trouble envisioning a lack of time and space. Physical beings are slaves to time and space. It seems that everything is put in one, the other, or both perspectives. I decided to see if Alec would elaborate on that.

"Alec, I am having trouble imagining a 'place' where there is no space or time. How does that happen?"

Alec's voice:

Think about having infinity such that you can be anywhere in infinity, but also many other places in infinity. It's hard to describe, but you can be on so many different planes at the same time, so space becomes meaningless. There is no physical 'space' or 'place.' Our vibrational levels are too fast to exist in any space and time continuum. And it is all intermingled because it's in infinity. Imagine having an infinite amount of storage on a computer server. And you can access it all in a nanosecond, if you know where something is stored. That's sort of what it's like.

Time is no longer a metric in infinity because it could be a millisecond or could be millions of years, and it's all the same. And like I said, our spirit vibrational level is so fast that it makes time meaningless. So when you are with other souls, it is not in the sense of one point in time, because they may be anywhere on the continuum of infinite time in the past, present, or future, and you may be as well. Therefore, time is meaningless.

"Can I meet you on another plane or in a different dimension sometime? How would I do that?"

Do you mean so that you can see me and not simply sense me? That would be difficult because mortals are very limited in what they can do in the multi-dimensional realm. My soul would have to become visible to you. It takes an incredible amount of energy. But rest assured, I am with you. I am all around you. Rest your eyes, your mind, your senses. I am there. You need to have no distractions, and truly open your mind.

"How do you experience the past, present, and future all at the same time? I'm not sure how you do that. Are there different planes or dimensions reflecting each one?"

We simply know. It comes to us. We may be on the present plane, and therefore we are in the present, and we know what happened in the past, and what will happen in the future. It's not something that we need to 'try to do' or need to find dimensions for. We know.

We are all connected with each other. A part of me is with Papa right now. Part of me is surrounding you. Part of me is with Vera, and with Dad, and with Nana. We are simultaneously everywhere we want or need to be. It's hard for physical humans to imagine that your soul can be with so many other souls at the same time. You didn't like physics much in college, but quantum physics helps.

Think of it as n-dimensional space. You can't see it, but you used it in your statistical learning. There are so many dimensions here. It's amazing when you first arrive, and it confused me at first. But it is so cool. I embraced it right away.

"How do you keep track of so many dimensions where your soul may be?"

You don't have to 'keep track'. You are, and you just know.

"I am seeing a vision of me sitting at my desk and a white light shadow of me gets up and goes to get water, and another shadow goes the other direction, and many shadows are coming out of my physical body, going in all directions."

Yes, does that help? I am trying to help you understand.

"Yes, it absolutely does help. I can envision it better now. So all those shadows are somewhere outside my physical body, seeing, and sensing, and being."

The shadows are reflections of different dimensions of your soul. And we can be an infinite number of them.

"How many dimensions are you in on a regular basis, Alec?"

So many, Mom, I cannot count them. You are starting to grasp the basics of it, though. You are learning!

I am not that enamored with the term 'afterlife.' It kind of suggests that there is no eternal infinite 'life,' because it's after the physical life. That's not at all true. I prefer other terms. They will come to you. Give it time. But afterlife is not a term I typically use. Heaven. Spiritual life. Eternal life. After physical life would be ok.

I don't think of 'afterlife' as a different realm, really. I am still very much aware of what is happening on the physical side, much more than I was when I was physically alive. I didn't keep up with the entire family when I was physically alive. I was only into me, and it was too much effort. I realize now how self-centered I was. I don't have regrets, because that is how I needed to be so that I would have the experience that my higher soul sent me to have. Things become much clearer after your physical body expires. You are aware of your own choices throughout your physical lifetime, and how those choices impacted others. For example, my choices with drug use greatly impacted you and Dad, and while I knew intuitively that it did, it wasn't until after I died that I really grasped how much.

The connectedness we feel as souls is something that is hard to explain, but you receive a great deal of 'knowing' when you first pass through the early stages of soul 'life' in this realm. It is like a lightning bolt of understanding. It is, and becomes, a part of your soul.

That bolt of understanding allows us to know things we didn't even experience on the physical side. An understanding of the physical side that surpasses what mortal beings currently know. This bolt of knowledge and understanding comes before you get to the learning cycle. You need it to be able to progress and exist as a soul, to understand your soul's journey, how things are all connected, and the infinity of simultaneous dimensions that are possible. Otherwise, you wouldn't understand the infinity of All. Nor would you be able to exist on the nonphysical side of things. Some souls understand, but still stay in a relatively small number of dimensions. Others, like my soul, explore too many to enumerate.

It's like crossing a bridge. Remember the rainbow bridge when Bucky and Lexi passed? On the other side of that bridge is a completely different realm, and you can't turn around and go back over the bridge. It's a one-way bridge. Once you step off that bridge, you get that bolt of understanding and knowledge, and you know how connectedness and infinite dimensions work. You don't know immediately how to be in many dimensions at once, but it's not long before you do. You naturally push a little to find your family and loved ones, and they surround you. You are soon connected to each one. They welcome you and embrace you with love and total acceptance. It's a wonderful feeling of all-encompassing love. You spend time with your family. I needed to learn 'who was who' and how we were connected on the physical side, but all I did was sense it. I knew.

Let's continue my journey. I am still in the learning infinity circle with many other souls, but we're on different layers of the circle. Many souls can be on a layer, or no souls. I am usually on a layer by myself because that is where I sense I should learn. It may be simply that it's where my divine spirits guide me. It doesn't matter if other souls are on the same level or not, because you don't interact with them or notice them while you are learning. You are intently focused on the 'silent movies' that play out to teach you. It's where I love to learn. I am learning so much. You can absorb so much knowledge by viewing these 'videos' instead of reading. Knowledge is becoming, and I am well on my way.

The way it works is that souls need to learn enough to be considered ready to move on to the next level of learning. It is infinite learning, but at some point, you are deemed ready to become one with your divine self. I am not sure when that is, because I'm obviously not there yet, but I am very happy, Mom. There is no boredom here. There is only joy and learning. Acceptance and family. Love.

Love is everything. Nothing here happens without love. When souls come together for something like a concert, we are all there with love and acceptance of others, and it is wonderful. The music fills me with joy and happiness, and I guess I would call it fulfillment. Like I don't want, or can't take, any more joy.

When Papa and I hang out, we 'talk' through our thoughts. Sometimes we get so excited that our thoughts cross and we are 'thinking' something at the same time. Does that sound like me, Mom? When we are together, we communicate about all kinds of things. Mostly about connectedness of everything to everything else. And the universe. How beautiful it is, and how wonderful it is knowing that God created such a beautiful and incredible universe. I often tell Papa about my exploring of other galaxies and what they are like. Mom-Mom loves my exploration stories, too, and so do the others in the family. Pop-Pop likes to hear how things work out there.

There is so much vastness and so many dimensions to explore, see, hear, sense, and understand. I am like a sponge. I also love that there are no tests or homework!

I am with you, too. Around you always, but often dormant. I am there in case you need me or talk to me. Like now, we are talking. I am right there with you.

I can see you typing. I am right next to you watching you type. I am trying to flow through your fingers like you asked the spirit guides to do. Do you feel me next to you?

"Yes, Alec, I feel you with me. I don't know where in the room you are, but it feels like you are on my right side."

Yes, Mom. I am! I am glad you are starting to sense me. Since I died, I have been with you, and with Dad, and with Vera. This is the first time you have really sensed me.

"I am starting to learn to let my mind go blank and let you in, I think. I love you, Alec."

I love you, too. I always have, but we need to work. I am glad you are in tune with me. That's it. Breathe and drink water. It will keep you going. It takes a lot out of you to do this.

I am going to try to describe how beautiful it is here, but it's very difficult because the beauty almost defies words. Even if you think of the most beautiful place that you've ever been, or ever seen in photos, it's so much more beautiful than that here. The colors are like nothing I've seen before. There are shades of blue and yellow and orange that are not imagined on earth. Human beings on the physical side think they have all the possible colors in their palette, but it's not true. And the unique, vivid colors can be part of our surrounding landscape in places not vibrantly colored on earth. Like rocks or mountains. Even water.

The surroundings are funny, because, like I said, there is no space and place. There are surroundings, or views, in the infinity continuum, and you can think your way to them. And to get back to your family of souls, you merely think about them, and then you are there with them.

"Do other souls also think themselves to other places?"

Yes, they do. We don't stay in one 'place' on the infinity continuum. We are in many dimensions or planes at the same time. A soul can stay with their loved ones on many planes and be exploring many other planes at the same time. It's hard to imagine, but I'm trying to explain the best I can.

"Does everyone get accepted there? Even murderers and robbers and people who are evil?"

Everyone has a reason for their experience in their physical life. Sometimes it is to experience what it is like to be evil. Those people have a heart and soul, too. In every human being's essence of their being, there is good, because God cannot create evil. Often, they are mentally challenged. Some are psychopaths and are driven to do the things they do because of their mental instability. They make choices, but often make the wrong one. Their divine soul likely determined that they needed to learn and experience some of that. I should mention that the higher beings and our Creator do not know of evil or negative things. God is pure and knows only of love.

You see, divine souls are made up of many, many lives, not all of which were good. There is a wide array of learning experiences that the manifestations of their soul have had. So yes, even so-called evil souls are welcomed back here, because they have completed their learning experience on the physical side. The physical side is so short compared to the infinity of time that exists here. Our divine souls know what experiences we need to complete our learning, and it involves good, evil, and mediocre. Rich and poor, brilliant and uneducated. All sides of mortal life.

"I see a cat. Is it Max? Missy?"

It's all cats. It's your sister's cat, your friend Kathy's in California, and your friend Becky's in Durham, all in one. The souls of animals are not unique. Each species has one soul. And when they return, they become part of the souls of all other cats, or dogs, or wolves, or horses.

Yes, Lexi and Bucky are both here. So are Brandy and Smoky, your cockapoo dogs from when you were young. They are part of the dog soul but can individually manifest as well. Your grandparents' dog, Boots, is here too. We all love our pets on the physical side. It's good because it gives them a wonderful life and ours is happier too, having them in it. It's hard when they die. It's hard when any close loved ones die, too. But that's what is so good about here, Mom. There is no death. We continue after our physical life; we do not die. We become part of everything.

You can learn how to do this more often. To connect with me and Papa and others. Then we can communicate more and more. I think it would help your anxiety.

"Yes, I feel so calm when I am in this state where I am receptive and can sense you. It's a clearing of the mind and letting go. The letting go feels nice."

Yes! And entering the afterlife is the ultimate letting go. You let go of all your fears, emotions, negativity, and physical ailments. All your pain, Mom. I saw you rotating your shoulder. All that will be gone. All you will feel is love, acceptance, and an eagerness to understand and learn.

"Do you ever see Jesus and saints? Do you see Higher Beings, like archangels?"

That's a hard question. It's not like we see them, but we know inherently they are there. I have tried to think about God and what it would be like to be in God's presence, but I have not learned enough, or become pure enough, to be worthy to be in His divine presence yet. Only Jesus has achieved that. God is everywhere and everything, though, and not only in one 'place.' So you can't really go to God. You embrace God in everything you do and every bit of love that absorbs you. Because God IS love.

"Why did you do drugs, aside from needing the life experience? What drove you to it?"

My physical self was too lonely and isolated. I was depressed, too. I wanted to escape, not be in my mind, not be in my body. I could not let it be. I ordered online and when it arrived, I was compelled to try it. When I tried it, I wanted more and more. Addiction is a craving that never stops. It haunts you. Even in recovery, it never fully went away. It was always there in the background.

"What else do you do in the afterlife, aside from learning and concerts?"

At concerts, there are many other spirits around and we all tune in and listen. We are closer to the spirits that create the music. The sound is clearer.

We spend a lot of time in the learning cycle. It is infinite and constantly evolving. We gather with friends or family and share our experiences. It's a little like Thanksgiving, but not only once a year. I sometimes share with them what I learn from you.

Other than that, I explore. A lot of that. I spend time with family. I'm learning about all your ancestors from Scotland and Germany, your Dad's ancestors from Sweden, Dad's from Slovakia and mine from Russia and eastern Europe. I can trace back to the first beings on earth. It's amazing.

Some of the other spirits play games, but I was never into sports. Remember you telling us that thunder was the angels bowling in heaven?

"Yes! It calmed you down during thunderstorms!"

Well, there are spirits that enjoy bowling, but of course, that's not what thunder is! Other spirits enjoy golf and other games. Sports are more limited because they rely on physical abilities, but they still exist. I was never much into any of that. But many spirits do partake in those activities because they enjoy it.

Like I said earlier, it isn't nearly as fun to play games when you know the future and how the game will end. I was always into technology and science, and now I can really see and start to understand the physics behind it all.

"Is there anything like movies for entertainment? Plays or acting? Or does knowing the past, present and future keep that from being entertaining?"

You're getting it, Mom. It's not very entertaining if you know what's going to happen next. There are some souls that enjoy acting, though. I was never into that. Everyone here has a different experience. What they enjoy now, and what they enjoyed on the physical side can be quite different. I enjoyed video games and coding on the physical side, and I can do that here if I want, but I don't like the violent ones I used to play. It's not the same as it was on the physical side. I have so much more understanding of how things work, and I can learn even more about that, which I enjoy.

I may try to learn a musical instrument. Not piano, but another instrument. I think I would like that. Maybe guitar or harp.

"That sounds wonderful, Alec. Would you have to store your instrument somewhere?"

Mom, you simply think about the instrument, and it will be in your hands. I don't need to physically store it. I'm not constrained by physical things because I can have what I need when I need it, by thinking about it. So I conjure it up.

My main responsibility is teaching. We all help each other continually as well. Part of the responsibility of the spirit world is to manage the mortals on earth. My role in that is mainly through a spirit teacher guide. While mostly I teach spirits, I can be sent to help guide mortals on their path on earth sometimes. The higher beings watch over each soul and its experience on earth, and they will dispatch the guides or spirits who are needed. The higher beings are messengers of God.

"Do you have apartments or possessions in the afterlife, Alec?"

There is no reason for me to have possessions, so I don't. I don't want to be 'tied down' by them. Some spirits like to have a few things, like musicians. Or those that play sports. Others have homes. I would rather be free to roam. And since there is no time or space here in the afterlife, it would be hard for me to have an apartment or something. Remember that I have told you that I am on multiple dimensions at the same time? I am not sure how I would have a place that would span that!

"Do you ever rest? Sleep? Do you have different moods in the afterlife? Do you ever get bored, tired, or grumpy? Or is it all positive, and various degrees of happy?"

It's more the latter, believe it or not. There is so much to learn. I couldn't possibly be bored, and there is no such thing as being grumpy. We are in a continual state of bliss.

We get a little tired or maybe overloaded is a better word, and then we pause whatever we are doing and rest. Sometimes that happens when I try to absorb too much learning all at once, but it happens infrequently. It's more that I get overwhelmed with knowledge and information. We don't have a physical body that gets fatigued or needs sleep. We are pure energy. So it is different from being physically tired, and we are always around. We are always learning and absorbing knowledge, and we have no sense of time, so it is constant.

You don't get bored or tired of this feeling of bliss and incredible love inside you. You want to bask in it and learn and understand. The feelings of joy, love, and acceptance stay with you all the time. It's so wonderful, I can't describe it. If you can think of a time when you felt pure joy, it's so much more than that.

We also have hope and aspirations. We aspire to be worthy of being in the presence of the higher beings, and ultimately to become one with Jesus, and with God. That is what we are working toward.

I must go now. We will continue tomorrow.

Cindy's voice:

I sat back and contemplated. I can't imagine a 'place' so beautiful, but that doesn't exist in space and time, and that you never bore of exploring. Something was bothering me, though. I was always taught that being bad and making bad choices meant I would go to hell. But it seems that everyone is loved and accepted if they are willing to receive that. God surely was the ultimate giver of love and forgiveness. But doesn't He judge our lives? Is there no Judgement Day?

He can't because He knows no evil or wrong. He only knows love. No payment for sins? Lots of questions were spinning in my mind.

CHAPTER 8

FILM AND VIEWS

Cindy's voice:

It's a hectic day and I need to present in a training course for a client in one hour.

Today's transcendental conversation may be brief, but I prayed to my higher self, my spirit guide, and all spirits of my divine self to guide me in my writing, to let the words flow through my fingers. I appeal to Alec's divine soul and spirits to help me tell the story that he wants to tell.

"Alec, what should we talk about today?" *Alec's voice:*

Books. Books on the physical side are hard to read. So many words take so much time to read. I was a slow reader too, so it took me even longer. I wish you could learn like we learn here, through thoughts; like movies playing. It is so much faster to learn that way. And you absorb so much more. Think about it. Maybe you should have a video to go along with the printed book you are writing.

"I'll think about how to do that. Maybe we could do it for certain sections. But I don't think I could figure out how to portray the colors."

You know what to do. You have connections that can help you. One is your massage therapist, who experienced death and returned.

She has the gift of seeing the colors of people. Another one did the artwork for the cover of a book. He had two near-death experiences, which inspires him to paint what he saw.

"Wow, Alec, that's a great idea. I'll think about that."

The colors here are intense and vivid. A video could show that well. Words can't.

"Will you help me get it right?"

I will try.

You know how you marvel at the sunsets, at the beach and in the mountains, especially? Think about that magnified with a sky that's an amazing blue, and the horizon, a beautiful hue of yellow and purple and some greens. That's one view I like.

There is another view of a sparkly green stream running through hills of medium to light muted yellow. The hills are not only one color. They are muted yellow, but also a warm brown and deep blue-purple here and there. The sky is a brilliant deep sky blue, but not dark, and is striped with clouds in different shapes. There are light orbs, which I know now are souls, which dot the sky here and there. The orbs have undefined edges, like they're blurred at the edge.

"Alec, what would you look like if I could see your essence, your soul? Would you be one of those orbs?"

How did I know you were going to ask that question? It doesn't matter what I look like, because we are all souls, and we all look the same.

We are differentiated by our senses. I can sense who Papa is, and Mom-Mom, and others. I know somehow from their emotional essence. But yes, I guess I would look like one of those orbs. Far away, like round orbs. Up closer, they can become more humanoid, but they blur and look like a blob from far away. I don't have a mirror here, Mom! And if I did, you know me. I wouldn't look at it.

I have been learning about galaxies, planetary systems, asteroids, meteors, and meteorites. Some of the stars you see at night are not stars, but rather planets in their stars' orbits, and I can see so many more planets that look like stars. Both in our own, and in other solar systems. Few of them have life, but they are exquisite and serve their purpose in balancing the universe. It's amazing to explore in what you call 'space' and beyond. I still remember what I learned in science classes about the planets, and still remember everyone wondered if there was life on other planets besides earth. There is Mom. But not like earthly mortals. I can't possibly explain it to you. They don't need suns and moons and oxygen to breathe, or even water to drink. So mankind may be looking in all the wrong places.

As an intermediate teacher, I teach other souls about the importance of understanding our true inner selves, and how to detach oneself emotionally when starting their life review. Otherwise, they hit roadblocks because of the emotions attached to events that happened in their lifetime. My detachment from my Asperger's in this past physical life helped me view things from a non-emotional, more objective focus, making it easier to get through much of this learning quickly. I am a teacher at the intermediate level because I was a teacher spirit long before my physical life with you, and I have grown and learned much since then. You'd be proud of me. I'm respected as an intermediate teacher, and many souls know who I am. I oversee a more junior teacher who does the main teaching, and I contribute some teachings as well and am there in case I'm needed.

"That's amazing, Alec. Do you teach anything else?"

Mom, isn't that enough? It's very important!

"Yes, I know that! I was just curious."

Yes, I know. You have always been curious, and so have I. I will be teaching about the inner self and what the expectations are for learning about the true inner self. It is so important to understand who you really are, and all your feelings and emotions. After you understand them, then you can work on the ones that are not pure of thought and love. The ones that are not in full acceptance of others. I also delve into how to understand the true self without becoming too emotional.

"Alec, I've always been proud of you. I wish I'd told you more often."

I know Mom. Don't cry because you will be on video teaching a class in a few minutes!

One other thing about the learning wheel. As you progress through the wheel, when you get to the next higher level of a topic, you may pass other souls who are still in that layer. I have passed many, so I know. They get stuck, not because they don't get the learnings, but because they are stuck with emotions, thinking about their loved ones back on earth. It's not that I don't think of you all, but I don't get stuck thinking about you. I think about you more when I'm with my family of souls.

I wish I could show you in a film or video what it's like in the learning wheel. It's huge. On the physical side, they would not fathom the magnitude in size. But again, there is no size, because there is no such thing as 'space' and 'time' here. Every particle of a circular layer in the learning center has a specific topic to learn. So it truly is like infinity times infinity times infinity.

Very few souls get through a single layer, much less several. I've managed to get through quite a few layers for many topics, but there are an infinite number of topics. It's not a race or competitive or anything. I'm an eager learner. Papa thinks it's great. He loves that I am eager to learn. He is too but goes a little slower and absorbs it deeply. Mom-Mom and Pop-Pop are on different topics. They spend a lot of time learning more about their families from Eastern Europe.

Tomorrow, Mom. I'll be here.

Cindy's voice:

I thought about what Alec was telling me about the learning and how he was able to get through so much learning so quickly. Alec was always very bright, and he learned quickly, especially about anything he cared about, or anything related to science or technology. When he was two years old, he could count backwards from two hundred.

At that age, he loved water towers and talking about how they stored water that went to all the houses, and watching the weather channel, especially the depictions of cold fronts in waves. I wondered if his fascination with weather and fronts was somehow connected to the afterlife and waves of information. It was all very confusing to this human.

ALEXANDER V. GIRMAN & CYNTHIA J. GIRMAN

CHAPTER 9

BLACK CAT

Cindy's voice:

We realized when the pandemic shutdown occurred, how incredibly lonely and isolated Alec must be. We were lonely and isolated initially, and we had a four-bedroom home with a dog and each other for company, and soon after shutdown, we were joined by our daughter Vera who came home from college. Early in the pandemic was scary enough as it was, with so little known about the virus and how it spread. With an older child five hours away that had executive functioning deficits and Asperger's, who was experimenting with drugs, it was even scarier. We could only imagine what it would be like to be in a tiny apartment twenty-four/seven like Alec had, especially with the hyperactivity of his ADHD.

Not only was Alec's office shut down, but the sober coach and outpatient program meetings went from in-person to virtual as the pandemic continued. He was spending almost twenty-four/seven in his tiny apartment, only leaving to walk, masked, down the block for groceries or fast food.

Alec still called, but not nearly as much as he did when he first moved to D.C. the prior summer. In fact, it was sporadic and typically the result of multiple voice mails and texts from us. When he finally would call, we would breathe a joint sigh of relief. Talking to him live was always a relief because he was alive. As the shutdown continued, Alec started to sound more and more low. We knew the loneliness and isolation were getting to him. It was so bad that even Alec admitted it. With his history of experimentation with hard drugs, that terrified us.

That's when we thought that it would be good for Alec to have a cat. He had always loved cats and dogs. A cat would be good company for him and give him the opportunity to take care of another living being. We found a small black cat that was purportedly three years old (we later suspected that it was only three months old). It was a cute cat and we adopted him on behalf of Alec.

Traveling to Washington, D.C. during the pandemic was eerie. D.C. was desolate. There was little traffic. Graffiti-plastered boards covered windows of business establishments that were empty and closed. Only a few restaurants were open, and those were drive-in or takeout. Our hotel initially looked closed, with the side doors locked and no valet or doormen around. There was only one main door unlocked in the front of the building. We walked in with our masks tight on our faces, covering our noses and mouths. The cat we were bringing to keep Alec company was in a carrier. He named the cat Chico and was excited on the phone and in texts about Chico coming.

The hotel receptionists looked at us suspiciously when we walked in. Then they checked us in, as if everything was almost normal. We were wary about the elevator. What if it was contaminated? Little was known about the COVID-19 virus and how it spread at this point. We almost held our breath as the elevator slowly chugged up to the sixth floor. We both breathed a sigh of relief when we saw the hallway was empty as the elevator door opened. We looked at each other without even speaking. We knew what each other was thinking. No one else around to infect us. We had not traveled anywhere since the worldwide pandemic had been declared.

Dropping our bags quickly in the room, we headed back downstairs to the car with cat in tow. The short drive to Alec's apartment was silent. My husband radiated apprehension, with his posture tense and his jaw set. My breath was shallow, and my heart was pounding as we drove. Even the cat meowed incessantly, not wanting another long trip in the car.

Alec knew we were coming. We had felt we needed to let him know because he had to get cat supplies. He was expecting us, and expecting the cat.

We got to the apartment building and rang the bell. We kept ringing until someone else came and let us in. Was he high? Was he passed out?

At his apartment, we knocked and got no answer. Eventually we tried the door, and it was unlocked. Alec was indeed passed out on the bed. It took some time and serious shaking to wake him. We were terrified when he wouldn't wake up. Finally he woke up, and all the fear turned to anger. He knew we were coming; yet he still got so high, he passed out? Was he trying to make us mad?

"What the hell are you thinking? Are you nuts?" Tom demanded.

"Alec, you knew we were coming this afternoon. Why would you do this?" I yelled.

Alec didn't respond. He tried to sit up but was disoriented. We waited a few minutes. Then the bombarding of questions began again.

"What did you do? What drugs did you take?" I asked.

We got no reply. That made me angrier.

Knowing that Alec didn't respond well to yelling, Tom tried to wave his hand to calm me down.

"What's up, bud? What's going on here?" he asked.

"I don't know," Alec responded.

"Have you been going to meetings? Have you been talking with your sober coach?" Tom asked.

"Yeah, I have. It's all on Zoom," Alec replied in a weary tone.

We had him call his sober coach and counselor to talk it out. They asked him good questions. You could tell by his tone that he didn't want to disappoint them. Still, he answered with one-syllable responses in a flat, monotonic voice.

After he hung up, we asked "Alec, are you really committed to recovery?"

"Yeah, I am," he responded. Of course, he said yes.

"How are we supposed to believe you?" I asked angrily. He was silent. My husband was patting the air with his hand as a signal for me to calm down. I was so angry that I didn't care if I was calm. I knew Alec didn't respond well to tension or yelling, but I couldn't help myself. It was so frustrating.

Once Alec was more awake and able, the three of us went to get something to eat. It was a silent and awkward dinner. I wasn't even hungry.

After dinner, we left Chico with him and went back to the hotel. We were worried and agonizing over how to help Alec. However, despite a thorough search, we hadn't found any drugs in his apartment, and we certainly couldn't all sleep in his tiny place. He only had a twin bed and didn't own a couch. Not that there was even room for one. Perhaps this would be a test of how well he could take care of a cat.

The next day, after a few calls, we drove over to Alec's apartment and went up, expecting to find him at his desk working. The door was unlocked when we arrived, and we walked into his tiny place and found him at his desk as expected. But there were drugs and drug paraphernalia all over the desk, and he was high yet again. He could barely coordinate his fingers to pick up a pen from his desk. It was infuriating.

"Idiot!" I yelled as I slapped the side of his head.

Tom just stared at him without a word. Alec just sat there. I was pacing frantically back and forth in the small living area. The recognition that he needed more intensive help hit us again like a ton of bricks. There was no backing away from that reality.

We asked him to call his sober coach again, and we got on the phone and discouragingly spoke to him about alternatives. He had some suggestions and was trying to be positive.

We moved Alec and the cat into the hotel with us. There was no way we could leave him on his own for another night.

We called the sober coach's top suggestion, and it was very expensive. We then called his insurance company to find out what residential treatment programs would take his insurance. We were on the phone between insurance and substance abuse residential programs the entire morning.

Finally, we found out that the sober coach's top choice would take his insurance. Of course, they only paid a small part of it. We drove Alec to Pennsylvania two days later, packing only what the residential program recommended and allowed. The drive was numbing, and everyone was mostly quiet. Any conversation was stilted and awkward, at best.

Alec was always eager to please, and although he reluctantly went along with the plan, his true feelings surfaced when he and Tom were waiting in the lobby to be checked in while I was out with the cat. Alec looked at Tom and said, "So you're basically locking me up in jail now." Tom responded, "You may feel that way now, but this is good program, and we hope you'll feel differently once it's done."

Instead of questioning his commitment, we put our faith in the program based on the sober coach's recommendation. We prayed it would get through to him.

CHAPTER 10

LOVE YOUR TRUE SELF

Cindy's voice:

It's a sunny day today, although the mountains are hazy. I pray to my higher self and spirit guide to guide me and help me write, giving me direction on the words to share with the physical side.

I appeal to Alec's higher self and spirit guides to allow the words to flow through my fingers. I am hoping for more clarity around all the questions that keep popping into my mind.

Alec's voice:

Time is not a factor here, as I've told you. It's hard to keep track of what happened when. We can only understand 'relative' time. Like, as I progress through the learning cycle, I can tell that I am passing other souls or finishing faster, but I don't know how long it took me or them.

I am not very clear about how long I've been here. I do know when it's the time of year that is important to you two, because I sense your sadness and you missing me. That calls me in. Like my Gotcha (Adoption) Day, my birthday, the anniversary of my death, and holidays when you are missing me even more than usual.

I sense you thinking about me a lot and tearing up. It's ok, but I don't want you and Dad dwelling on me all the time. You're doing it now - tearing up. It's time to start living your life as if there are no tomorrows. You have so much more life to live. Get outdoors. Enjoy nature. Hike. Go on your birding and safari trips.

When I was on the physical side, I didn't understand all the trips you and Dad took to go look at birds. I thought you guys were crazy. Now I understand much more. Every living thing is so beautiful and should be appreciated. God created a beautiful earth that you live on, so many things of beauty to see. Most people can only see a fraction of them in their lifetime, but you should see as much as you can and truly appreciate it. Bask in the beauty. Try to understand it. Feel the beat of the wings as they fly when you're birding. Absorb the colors and the unique features of every bird.

The same with landscape and scenery. You love the mountains. They make you feel at home because it's where you grew up. But what about all the other mountain ranges all over the world? Each one is unique and should be seen and enjoyed. If you still skied, it would be a great way to appreciate the mountains, but hiking is good too.

And waterfalls and streams. Rivers and seas. All of them make up the world that God created for mortals to enjoy in their physical lives. It's unfortunate that it's being destroyed, and much faster than humankind appreciates. But let's not go there.

I have no regrets about my life as I've said because it played out exactly as it was supposed to. I experienced what I was meant to. I was meant to be born to a birth mother that was an addict, to better ensure that I would have the experience of addiction myself. Often those with addiction or family with addiction struggle with mental health. So it is no surprise that I did. My Asperger's made me seem 'quirky' to others and awkward socially. I was constantly trying to hide my quirks in public so that I would fit in. I realize now that I could have been myself and had the same friends. But I was meant to spend a lot of time alone, to be lonely and isolated and seek friendship with drugs.

I know it's hard for you to hear these things, but try to accept them as facts. I was predestined to be exactly who I was, like you are predestined to be who you are. You have choices though, so think about them as you go through your life. You'll spend a lot of time reviewing all those choices someday!

Since we are talking a lot about the physical side, I want to tell you that my life with you as parents was a good one. You were good parents. You did the best you could. Yes, there are things you could have done differently. Everyone has that. Specific instances where you might have handled things differently or had a different reaction. I was very sensitive to Dad's outbursts because I was very sensitive to yelling. But that's the way he is made, Mom. I don't think you and Dad appreciated how much sensitivity I had until I was diagnosed with Asperger's. Before I was diagnosed, remember you used to ask me to look you in the eye when you spoke to me? Of course, that's a classic Asperger's symptom, but you didn't know that until after the diagnosis and you looked it up.

"Yes, Alec, I wish I'd known so much earlier. And I wish I'd read the book by John Elder Robison called 'Look Me in the Eye' (Crown, 2007), because it explained so much about Asperger's from someone who experienced it every day. It would have helped us understand you so much more."

It's ok Mom. It is what it is, and I had a good life.

I have mentioned the higher beings and how every divine soul is trying to become one with them. I don't think I mentioned the light that surrounds the higher beings. It is intense. It is so bright that it serves as a background light for all of us souls, even though it's far away. Sort of like the light of the moon when it's more than half full. And they are all around us.

We all aspire to earn our oneness. Becoming one with our higher self. Then becoming one with higher and higher beings and ultimately God, which requires purifying ourselves of anything that is not love. Why do we have to earn it? Why do we have such aspirations when we are so happy?

We exist in a constant state of bliss, total acceptance, and love. We have no doubts about whether another soul likes us or what they think of us. There are no secrets here. Thoughts are open and known. We know other spirits love us and accept us unconditionally. It's important therefore for us to have something to aspire to. If we didn't, our eternity might eventually become stale, despite the blissful state of love and acceptance. It is always good to have hope. Hope is an underappreciated feeling on earth. Love and forgiveness and hope are all you need.

It's especially important to forgive yourself, to love yourself. Too many mortals go through life being dissatisfied, even disgusted with themselves, which causes them to not be able to love others fully. Because they do not love themselves, they are cynical of life and unappreciative. It's possible to love yourself but have too much greed and egotism such that you can't love anyone else—no one seems good enough. But in most cases, you can love others because you have accepted and love yourself. There are exceptions, though.

You could learn to love and accept yourself more, Mom. It's why you have a lot of anxiety and insecurities. When you finally accept the true you, you will be amazed at how most of those anxieties fall away. You've always tried to be what everyone else wants, or what you think would impress others. You've accomplished a great deal that way. You will soon learn who you are, and what you really want to do for the rest of your life. Who you want to be.

Dad should also spend more time learning to accept and love himself. Both you and Dad grew up in a home of love, but you both had fathers who were not around a lot, and you both always wanted their acceptance. I see it clearly in both of you. Be assured that both of your fathers are exceedingly proud of you and love you immensely, more than you can imagine.

I am not trying to tell you how to live your lives, now or in the future. I'm just trying to pass on some of my newfound wisdom. You'd be very proud of all I have learned. Now I can appreciate how much you two loved me and why you did some of the things I didn't understand when I was living. You and Dad both wanted to save me from going down the path I chose. I know that now.

Back then, I thought you were trying to control me. I appreciate all that you did for me.

It's hard to join you in those medium sessions sometimes. I need to relive my life some to be able to communicate with the physical side and I must communicate through someone I don't know. In other words, a little bit of my Asperger's comes back, I guess because I'm talking with a stranger, and I must come down to the earthly vibrational frequency to be able to communicate.

"You'd probably feel better if you were talking about technology!"

Yes! That's true Mom. I could always talk to anyone about that. But feelings, events, past mistakes—all those things are very difficult conversations to have.

"You don't have to have those conversations if you don't want to. But I need you to help me tell your story. That may bring up memories that aren't pleasant for you. Will you help me?"

Yes, I will as much as I can. I like telling my story to you; it's strangers that are hard to talk with.

When I was in Washington, D.C., it was the first time I was living on my own. I know it was a tiny place, but it was my apartment, my own place. I started off being kind of lonely, but then I started exploring D.C. That was nice. I'd go for long walks and ride the metro to see places and sightsee. Sort of funny how I'm exploring still.

But then, I got bored and lonely as time passed on. I went to work every day, and I enjoyed the job, but the evenings and weekends dragged on. I started experimenting with drugs. Of course, I did that before with pot and my ADHD medication, even stealing some of your pain and sleep medications, as you remember. But I hadn't experimented much with other stuff.

I don't remember how I came across crystal meth the first time online, but it sounded like something I wanted to try. I ordered what I thought was a little, but because it was so cheap, it was a large amount. Well, once I got all that, I had to use it all up. And that's when it started. I was totally high when I came to Roanoke for holidays that year.

You and Dad were oblivious. You were so happy to see me, so you couldn't 'see' what was going on with me.

You came to D.C. not long after that for a business trip. Luckily, I knew you were coming. We went out to a nice dinner, and then you came back to the apartment. You made me clean the apartment because it was such a mess and I hated that! I hid the hard stuff well, but I forgot about the pot in my backpack. You made me throw it out. But I was the one that took it to the dumpster, so I hid it along the way. I was sneaky about the drugs. I probably could have gotten pot through a prescription because of my ADHD and Asperger's, but it was easier to get online.

"I figured you'd not toss out any of the pot, but because it was becoming legal in so many states, I was conflicted. Right or wrong, I also felt it was better than some of the serious drugs you were using."

There was nothing you could have done to save me. I can sense your guilt. Even if you moved to D.C. and shared an apartment with me, I still would have found a way. And it was meant to be that way.

I am honored that you co-write this book about me and my journey and impressions of the afterlife. I like the idea of people understanding my story. Don't portray me as a helpless boy with a disability, Mom. Portray me as a man, with the strength to live with Asperger's and ADHD and a job I loved, doing what I loved to do - coding. Portray me as strong in my recovery for twenty months. I am also happy that you want to portray what it's like here. People need to have hope and not be so terrified of dying. You don't die, you simply transform into a spirit being. You retain your memories and your personality, only without a physical shell.

Let's talk about things you don't know already. Maybe during your conversations with me you should play heavenly music to get in the mood lol. See if SIRI or Alexa know any celestial music.

Yes, that's it. Spa type music is what we hear. Softly in the background.

Now that we have the music background, you can close your eyes and get a sense of what it might sound like in the afterlife. And I can communicate better through this frequency. Also, it's later in the morning. I do my best earlier - maybe earlier tomorrow and you can go back to sleep afterward!

"I'll try Alec!"

So now, let's talk about other senses. We've talked about what I see and how beautiful it is here, with colors that are not seen there on the physical side. We've talked about the love and acceptance I feel and sense with my soul, and how I am filled with bliss and unconditional love and acceptance. We've talked about how we communicate, that it's not through voice but rather through thought and emotion. Let's talk about smell and touch. Well, we don't have to spend much time on smell because I don't smell much of anything. But let's talk about touch. I was always sensitive to textures. Remember I would never dry myself with a towel, I would only air dry? And I couldn't stand the texture of jeans or certain other fabrics on me. I wanted to wear super soft clothes.

Here, there is no touch. If you touch something, your essence goes through it. That's sort of like the ghost myth that you've seen in movies and cartoons. We aren't physical as souls, so you lose those senses. But you gain so much more.

There are senses that human beings don't have on the physical side. Like the 'knowing' of things when you haven't 'learned' them yet. And knowing of historical things that you haven't experienced. You know things from your prior lives, too. All that knowing sort of happens. When you want information, it pops into your head. It took a lot of getting used to, but it's really cool.

We hear and feel and smell things from memories, though. If we are thinking of a memory, those senses can be tapped as part of memory, but we don't otherwise have those senses here. The memories keep those senses alive, because we all miss being able to smell and anticipate the taste of a good meal, or really feel the sensation of a hug.

"How do you hug in the spiritual realm, Alec?"

Here we connect with each other and then we 'know' each other. It is a joining of our memories and emotions, and it feels fulfilling and wonderful. There are only positive emotions, no pain, no despair, no sadness. So it is like a feel-good movie, only multiplied by infinity. It is the ultimate sensual experience with those you love. It is not sexual. We will always be with each other that way. For now, I am there around you. So are Papa and Mom Mom, your grandparents and all your many aunts and uncles. Friends of yours that passed are with you, too. You simply need to call on them and they will be there for you.

The most powerful feeling here is the incredible emotional sensing of love, all around us.

Until tomorrow, Mom. Earlier, ok?

Cindy's voice:

Alec mentioned that learning to love yourself was critical and fed directly into being able to truly love others. I wondered when I would be able to forgive myself for not recognizing what was going on with Alec during his childhood and teenage years. While it seems clear now, there were so many signs I missed along the way because I was so wrapped up in myself - my job, the business traveling, our social life, our marriage. Alec was diagnosed with ADHD in kindergarten, but it wasn't until much later that the diagnosis of Asperger's came. Had we known earlier, we may have been able to get him help in developing coping skills. But he was saying that he was meant to have the life he had, that it was predestined. We loved Alec fiercely and unconditionally. I needed to let my guilt go and forgive myself. He lived the life that was intended and he himself said he knew how much we loved him and that we were good parents. Hearing that from heaven meant the world to us.

ALEXANDER V. GIRMAN & CYNTHIA J. GIRMAN

CHAPTER 11

EXPLORING THE UNIVERSES

Cindy's voice:

A beautiful sunny day. But not that early.... I should have set my alarm. I pray for forgiveness to Alec's higher self and spirit guide and ask them for guidance and help in writing this morning. I pray to the spirit guide of my higher self for the same. Guide me and let the words flow through my fingers.

"What are you doing while you wait for me to start our conversation, Alec?"

Alec's voice:

I am everywhere and in everything, so there is not one 'doing' activity. I do not wait for you. I am in thousands of dimensions having thousands of experiences. You see, a spirit is energy, and the speed of spirits is light. Because the vibrational level of spirits is so fast, spirits can be everywhere almost simultaneously, at least at the higher being spirit level. However, even though my vibrational level as teacher spirit is lower, the difference would be indistinguishable from mortals. A tiny part of me watches to see when you are ready.

You were not early this morning, Mom. I think you and I were a lot alike that way. I loved to sleep in the mornings.

A part of me is in another universe discovering, parts of me are exploring different views and dimensions of the afterlife, parts of me are in the learning cycle, learning different topics. Part of me is with Papa and part of me with other relatives and ancestors. It's so fascinating to learn about our different ancestors and their role throughout the history of humankind.

"I had a dream last night that was not pleasant. I was being chased by someone that would not give up. I have these sorts of dreams often. Do you know why?"

It's your anxiety, Mom. Like I said earlier, try to learn more about meditation and self-awakening. Self-love. It will help. And your medications can sometimes cause nightmares.

"Do you ever visit me in dreams, Alec?"

Yes, but you hardly ever remember.

"What does it look like in other galaxies and universes, Alec?"

I can't describe that. It's all so very different. Some planets are desolate, like the moon looks through a telescope, with the craters, rifts and gulleys. Others are smooth, still others have mountains and plateaus, and you wonder what is inside of them. When I wonder, often the answer pops into my head. One planet existed with a whole infrastructure inside of it I could explore!

"Is there life on another planet in one of the universes?"

It depends on what you define as life. Mortals can't even define that on earth.

"Well, that's true. I guess it's not the need for oxygen, but rather something that grows and thrives."

Many things grow on earth that aren't considered 'life' on earth. Think about mountains and glaciers. Over time, they add mass. Is that life?

"I see what you mean, Alec. It's hard to define. But you have lived the physical life of a human being on earth. Is there anything even comparable to that life out there?"

Not quite. But there are intelligent beings, far more intelligent than mortals, that thrive on planets that are too far away for mankind to reach with their current technology.

"Do you think our technology will advance enough someday to allow communication with them?"

It's more likely that they will communicate with mankind on earth than mortals reaching them. In fact, they have. But only certain mortals know and are receptive to it. Almost like communication from the afterlife. I wonder how many mortals mistake communication from spirits as communication from 'aliens' and vice versa. Something to think about.

"How do you split up parts of your soul to go wandering and exploring here and there?"

It's not something I have to try to do. I merely think it. I just wonder. I have always been curious, you know that. It's what got me into trouble on the physical side.

"Yes, curiosity about chemistry and electricity - what combining different chemicals would do or doing certain experiments with your electricity kit and almost causing a fire!"

Yes, my initial experiments with drugs were really driven by curiosity about chemicals. I was taking chemistry at the time. I found your medications and started looking up what they were and what they would do to me.

"We should have kept them locked up."

Mom, no guilt. I would have found them somehow. It was meant to be, and how were you to know that I would be searching your bathroom drawers when you were out?

Here, curiosity is how we learn. Some souls are naturally more curious than others, and so they go through the learning topics at a quicker pace so that they can move on to another topic. We learn what we want to learn. I don't have to learn different languages because there is no language here. We all 'speak' the same language because the thought is the concept, not the words. We communicate emotions through feeling of the emotions, again not words. And concepts are communicated through visions.

In fact, the transcendental conversations are hard because I must translate into words and that is draining. It's so much easier to communicate here with others through thought and emotion. Effortless.

"Alec, is there a hell? Have you glimpsed hell?"

We all have glimpsed a dark side with negative emotions that we do not want to experience, so we keep away. Sometimes plans of our higher selves go awry. A single soul can become greedy and no longer want to be part of their higher divine self. They want to create a new higher self that is evil and not loving. You can see where I'm going here, right?

I mentioned earlier about how mortals with mental health conditions can turn to crime, such as psychopaths, that are driven to commit murder and do other harm and violence. When they pass, they are met with love and acceptance as well as forgiveness by their relatives and their higher self, like all of us other souls.

Some souls do not want that bliss and love. They balk at the welcoming. Instead of being willing to accept what they did in their human shell, admit their sins and accept the forgiveness and love, they want to immediately go back to the physical living. They don't love themselves. They don't want to die, but it is often too late. They have a lot of anger and hate, even though their mental health conditions have fallen away. They do not want to return to becoming part of their higher self and they fight being in the afterlife, instead of accepting it. They can't continue as their own soul. It's against God's law. I don't know exactly because I don't dwell on it, but I know it has something to do with the darker place. They are not burned. You cannot burn energy. I think maybe they are remodeled or rehabilitated. Some may call this hell. But it may not be eternal. They may reach atonement and forgiveness and come back to the blissful state.

Don't get me wrong. That doesn't mean that spirits coming to the afterlife don't need to atone for their wrong-doings. There is an in-depth evaluation of all the choices made in the physical life and an opportunity to atone for choices that were not the best. The point is to learn from those choices. Remember that there may have been a reason for them to have the specific life experience that they had.

But most souls who come to the afterlife experience the love and blissfulness of total acceptance and they want to be part of it. They remember all their past lives and their intent of their last physical life as a learning experience.

Mom, tell Aunt Kathy that I love her too. She was always telling me she loved me. Remember? She always said, "Have I told you today that I love you?" If by text, I would ignore it. And I didn't like talking on the phone. So I hardly ever responded to her. But that was my Asperger's, not my soul. I really did love her. You and Dad too. And Vera and Nana and Mom Mom, all the relatives and all your friends. I couldn't express it when I was on the physical side, except to you and Dad. Now I can.

As I have tried to communicate, our souls, once we pass, can watch the experiences of other souls that are part of our divine self, and our loved ones and relatives. It really gives us a good sense of what is going on with the physical side, but I can't see every mortal on earth. There are some souls who have that gift. My soul needs some sort of connection, and I have a connection to many mortals, but not to all of mankind. When I say I am connected to everything, it doesn't mean every physical being on earth. But I do feel connected to all the mountains and lakes, streams and forests, oceans and plains. Also, all the butterflies and birds and living things that are not human beings. I suppose if I tried hard enough, I might be able to be connected to more mortals, but I have too much to learn about all kinds of other things first. Because I am connected to so many humans, I can see how your lives are progressing and sense what is happening on the physical side.

"If you are with me sometimes, how do I know? Do you ever give me signs?"

All the time, Mom. All the time. But you don't recognize most of them as signs.

"How can I recognize them?"

Become more aware and in tune with yourself and you will recognize them, I promise.

"Was it a sign when I found those two dimes within the same hour?"

Yes, that was a sign. A positive sign when you found out you were going to meet with the professor about transcranial alternating current electrical stimulation for treatment of substance use disorders and about doing studies.

"Thank you for those signs. They mean so much to me."

The veil is thinner when it's earlier in the day. Right before dawn or during sunrise is the best time for these transcendental conversations. I must go now. Shall we meet again tomorrow?

"Yes, son, let's do."

Cindy's voice:

Being in thousands of dimensions simultaneously, intelligent life on another planet far, far away, and remodeling of souls that are uncooperative or evil. My mind was about to explode!

Will I ever understand all of this? Probably not while living on the physical side, but I'd at least like to understand the concepts and I'm definitely not there yet!

ALEXANDER V. GIRMAN & CYNTHIA J. GIRMAN

CHAPTER 12

IN SEARCH OF SOBRIETY

Cindy's voice:

Alec was, at times, difficult to understand. He didn't express his emotions to others. He did occasionally express himself to us as his parents, but on the rare occasions that he did, it was with hesitation and reluctance. It was often difficult to tell what he was thinking. He often didn't get sarcasm or jokes because most people with Asperger's take language literally. Direct questioning sometimes got us answers but sometimes got us single syllables like "Yeah" or "OK" or "Good". I'm sure that happens with other parents, too.

During the intense thirty days he spent in the Pennsylvania inpatient residential program, Alec wasn't allowed to call us except once a week, on Sundays, and only on monitored house phones with residents waiting in line to use them, so he couldn't talk long. They weren't allowed to make calls on their personal phones, which were locked away in the main office with their laptops and other electronic devices. The communication wasn't nearly enough for us, and I don't think it was for Alec either.

At the end of the Pennsylvania inpatient residential program, the counselors did not think Alec was ready to be on his own. We found a longer-term program at a sister facility in Boca Raton, Florida, and purchased a one-way flight. We couldn't see him–rules of these intense residential rehab programs. They took him to Philadelphia airport and made sure he got on the flight, and someone met the plane in Miami and took him to the facility. Again, no laptops or phones were allowed except for one supervised phone call a week with us. He started the program, and we heard little about progress at first. Alec was laid off from his job in D.C. not much later.

Once Alec was transferred to the inpatient program in Boca Raton, we started having weekly family counseling with him while he continued intense one-on-one counseling and group sessions. I'm not sure how to describe those family sessions. They were simultaneously awkward, emotional, frustrating and helpful and we made little progress in two months.

It was all very expensive, and we didn't feel like Alec was fully committed. After two months, he transferred to a somewhat looser residential program in Raleigh that allowed visitors. He finally started working hard, and we made progress in our family sessions, too. We weren't sure what caused the change, but having counselors he could relate to and a little more freedom despite the continued structure may have contributed.

This program allowed the use of a computer in free time. Alec loved to code and would do it just to have a challenge. He would code bubble sorts from scratch, just to make sure he understood what a bubble sort was and how to accomplish it. He did a lot of coding like that and found it fun.

The program also had built-in career time for studying or applying for jobs. We started feeling a bit of hope. We started intensive family therapy in August. We used a nice work booklet for these sessions that asked probing questions about our relationship with Alec, and his with us. It helped prompt some deep thinking about our relationship and style of communication. It was eye opening to hear how some of our actions were interpreted and the impact they had on our son. It was also surprising how Alec was so willing to be open. We had thought we were being good parents. He had interpreted those actions as trying to control him. He found some insight into how his actions impacted us as well. These sessions really helped our communication styles and our relationship with Alec, and we were able to talk more freely among the three of us. We will forever be grateful to his counselor Emily for that.

Four months after starting the residential program in Raleigh, Alec landed a programming (coding) job. A panel conducted the first of two planned interviews for the position with Alec by video call and he was to respond to questions verbally and use the Zoom white board feature. As part of the interview, he would be asked to show how he would approach a coding task. He had spent a bit of time looking at standard types of interviews for coding jobs, and all the websites said to make sure to repeat the task back in your own words and ask clarifying questions so that you understand exactly what the task is and the assumptions to be made. Alec did just that and then wrote out the code without hesitation on the whiteboard. Alec said that they were so impressed with him that the panel looked at each other at the end of the call.

"I don't think we need to interview him again. I think we know he is intelligent and highly skilled. He has what we need," one of them said.

The job offer came a week later, and he started a week after that. All of us were ecstatic. This was exactly what we had hoped for. Alec enjoyed programming so much that it wasn't work for him. To have your job be something you do for fun is a dream!

Alec did well in the job and in the residential recovery program. Five months after starting the Raleigh intensive rehabilitation and therapy program, he moved to a transition house with three other guys from the residential program. The counselors paid surprise visits to the house frequently and continued random drug tests, but the four guys were able to enjoy more freedom while still participating in group activities and counseling. Things seemed to be going quite well.

Alec continued to bring up a car and an apartment in our family sessions. We had fears about both. However, it was clear that he would need a car when the shutdown lifted, and staff started working again on site. We didn't feel he was ready for an apartment. In March, Alec found a good deal on a used rental car that was fully loaded with extras. He was so excited to do his own research, apply for his own loan and get all the paperwork done and out of the way before the pickup. He came to visit us in the mountains a few weekends later, driving the new car, and took us for a ride on the Blue Ridge Parkway in western North Carolina. It was a beautiful spring day, and we saw two black bear cubs frolicking in the grass on the side of the road. I'll never forget it. We had a great visit, more relaxed than it had been in quite a while.

About five weeks later, on a Friday night around 10:00 pm, I got a call on my cell from Rex Hospital Emergency Room Services. We were alarmed. The police had brought Alec to the Emergency Room because of a car accident. They were quick to assure me he was not injured, and no other car was involved, but that it was clear that he was inebriated. His car was totaled.

We were relieved that he was uninjured, but our worry and anxiety about his sobriety went into overdrive. Alcohol had never been his drug of choice. It was surprising, therefore, that this would happen, and we wondered if it reflected desperation.

Alec claimed he had just been 'curious.' but clearly recovery had reached a big hurdle. Alec was learning to "adult" and he did his research, and lawyers were contacted. Court date was set. It was a very anxious time for him as well as for us as parents.

Our family sessions continued, and we expressed these worries, while at the same time, Alec was expressing wanting to be in his own apartment. He started looking and found an apartment he liked in a complex that would allow him to walk to groceries and a few restaurants. We finally recognized that there was little we could do to stop him. He certainly could afford an apartment with his salary.

He took possession of the apartment in mid-June but didn't move in until July 4th weekend, so that he could get more intensive counseling before move-in, mostly due to his Driving Under the Influence (DUI) charge and accident. He was excited, and we finally tried to see this as a big step in accountability and responsibility. We were suppressing our worry for the time being. Alec kept in touch with us regularly, and the communication and family sessions continued. He seemed committed to his sobriety and recovery and his job was going very well. He had figured out the bus schedules and was going back to Raleigh for counseling and meetings.

In early to mid-July, the firm where Alec was working started to bring people back to work. They held a grand opening of their new office space in Durham, not far from Alec's apartment, and Alec was truly excited about being part of that and going into the office a few days a week to work. However, each time they tried to bring people back to the office, an outbreak would cause them to back off. They finally shut back down toward the end of July. We didn't realize, given the meetings and counseling back in Raleigh, that Alec was becoming isolated and lonely again. He was also frustrated about not going back into the office. He had enjoyed his brief time with colleagues.

August was a busy month for us. We had planned for Alec to come visit, but he said he was not feeling well. Although we were still talking on the phone and having family meetings monthly, we didn't get back to visit him until early October.

We were going through Durham on the way to my nephew's wedding and offered to take Alec out to lunch at one of his favorite restaurants. We had a nice lunch with him, although he seemed distracted. He enjoyed his big burger, fries and coca cola.

On our way back from the wedding, we didn't tell Alec ahead of time that we might stop by his apartment. We just texted him when we were about ten minutes away. It was a short and frustrating visit. There was no denying Alec was high, even though he vehemently denied it to us. We knew he was. The signs and symptoms were there. He could hardly string words together for sentences, and his coordination was poor. We left aggravated, and once on the highway, immediately called his counselor.

His counselor contacted Alec that Sunday, then went to his apartment the next day to obtain a urine test for a drug screen. His urine was clean. We knew something strange was going on because he had clearly been high. We would later learn that clean urine can be bought online, and even warmed against the body if someone knows they'll be tested.

On Tuesday night, we spoke with Alec by phone, and he was excited about coming to visit us at the beach for the coming weekend, although we couldn't reach him Wednesday, Thursday or Friday by text or phone.

CHAPTER 13

VIEWS FROM THE AFTERLIFE

Cindy's voice:

Much earlier this morning and still dark outside, I pray to my spirit guide and other spirits of my own divine self and of Alec's divine self to give me direction and allow the words to flow through me to these pages.

I went to an art show and there, met an artist that did beautiful paintings with wax. I asked her what her inspiration was. She said it simply came to her. She never knew what she was going to paint. "Are you clairvoyant?", I asked. She said, "Yes, a bit", and looked at me curiously. I said that I had visited psychic mediums and since then, experienced some visions that reminded me of some of her paintings, especially the ones that looked like a path leading to some distant place. She asked if she could hug me. I hold on to these visions and voices from heaven with all my heart.

Alec's voice:

Mom, hold on to those visions. I am sending them so that you can understand. In earlier sessions, I described several views that I've seen here that are so beautiful. You asked what most of the afterlife looks like. I can't answer that because there is no '*most* of the afterlife'. It's all so different depending on what you are thinking about. When I try to explore, I am drawn to certain views and topics that come to mind, or that I've been learning about. They are there for me to discover and learn about when I think about them. But it's rare that I am not thinking of something. Especially as part of the learning process. When I am learning, I am totally absorbed in a topic and what is related to that topic is what my soul's eye sees.

When I visit family and ancestors, the background is subtle. Because I am visiting with other souls, I don't notice a vibrant scene. It's more the way it is right before dawn, like now. A little hazy and slightly dark. The brightness of the souls of my family dominates the background.

When I think of mountains, like those where you are now, I see mountains. Not exactly like the Blue Ridge Mountains of North Carolina, but mountains, nonetheless. Almost like what an abstract painter would portray and with different muted colors, with splashes of more vibrant colors amongst the mountains. Rolling mountains like you see out the window.

When I think of bodies of water, I see oceans or lakes that are sparkling in the light, sometimes surrounded by hills, other times by flat land with rocks or sand. Always in colors that are vibrant and not like on earth. Although some colors are soft pastels. More like how an older child might color in an outlined picture with colored pencils, staying in the lines.

Within the learning wheel, there is nothing to see except the topics in front of us, and they bring up portrayals of whatever we are learning about. It is amazing.

We need no sustenance, other than love. And learning when we are at that phase. I like concerts because they give me such joy. Music does that for me now. Remember, I used to not like much music when I was in my physical life? I found much of it too vocal and too whiny. But the instrumental music here is beautiful. Others may hear different music that they enjoy. I never thought much about that.

I sometimes miss taste. Especially the taste of cheeseburgers and chocolate cake. But we don't need any food and it's not something we crave, like I craved drugs. Instead, it's a nice memory of sorts.

I was thinking about what we talked about the other day. About people that don't live good lives on the physical side. Forgiveness of all your wrongs happens immediately by others here. Spirits also have to forgive themselves and that can take time. They may spend a lot more time in the initial phases described earlier in our sessions. It's the 'in-between' place. Everyone is given that chance of forgiveness and self-love, and of acceptance for who their true soul really is, which may be very different from what they were on the physical side.

"When you get to the afterlife, how do you know where to find your divine soul?"

You are drawn to yourself because it is you. Your divine soul is completely you, and you are completely your divine soul. That's a little like asking how you find yourself when you wake up in the morning on the physical side. Do you see what I mean?

Every soul has their own divine soul that they return to after their experience on the physical side. That experience on the physical side is to learn some sort of lesson or lessons. There may be multiple lessons involved in one physical lifetime. And multiple accomplishments and impacts that one physical human may have on mankind. Once they return from their learning experience, they will reconnect their divine soul and all their past incarnations and experiences. However, they cannot become one with their divine soul until they have learned maximally from their physical life experience.

Even though you may think you aren't having an impact on mankind, you are in subtle ways. Every mortal life is. The people that you interact with take away something from those interactions. Think about that movie "It's a Wonderful Life" that plays around Christmas. He touched so many lives and without him, things would have been so different. He received the gift of being able to see what life would have been like if he hadn't been born. It's the same with you and with Dad, and with all humans. You are having much more of an impact than you know, and when you enter the afterlife, you'll be able to review and understand that in detail. You'll be able to see what your life would have been like if you made different choices.

You hear the wind blowing the leaves outside your window? Yes, I am the wind. I am the rain and clouds. I am with you. As are all your relatives who have passed.

"Do they know about our transcendental conversations, Alec?"

Yes, they do. They are proud and excited about it.

"Tell me about my ancestors, if you can."

You have a lot of ancestors. There is no one description. The relatives that you knew in your lifetime are a good representation, though. Your ancestors extend far back in time, and you wouldn't recognize the ones from then. Human beings in early Sweden, Scotland and Germany didn't look like they do today.

"Is anything scary about the afterlife, Alec?"

Nothing is scary here. We are all accepted and loved. We have no fears. There are souls that are more eager to learn and explore than others. The same as on the physical side. It's so freeing here. Even those that were lazy or uninterested in learning on the physical side are fascinated with learning here because all the physical struggles are gone.

It's exactly like you to ask about things that scare you, Mom. Your anxiety is higher than when I was alive physically. Do something about it before it gets too bad.

"How can there not be time, Alec? How can things 'progress' without time?"

It's hard to describe, but there isn't a sense of time because of the infinity aspect of things. There is no rush to meet a deadline. No push that you should do something in a certain timeframe. We learn and visit and exist in infinity.

"What else do you do in the afterlife besides learn, explore the universe, visit soul groups and go to concerts?"

We watch over our loved ones on the physical side. We share with each other. We love and support one another.

Some souls have special interests. Mine is science and technology. Sometimes I will find special learnings on those. I share with Papa about some of those. He enjoys hearing about them. He likes learning. Mostly he loves being free, especially free of dementia and heart disease.

Chico is in your office with you. I miss my cat. But I am with him too.

"What about the portrayal of angels historically? In many of the paintings that date back hundreds of years?"

Angels seem to always be portrayed with wings and long robes with a sash. Sometimes with harps. The harp is a beautiful instrument and sometimes we hear that playing. The rest was the imagination of those on the physical side long, long ago. We don't see angels that way.

"Can you see angels and spirit guides of other divine souls?"

If I try to separate them, sometimes I can. But we don't really differentiate so much here. They are part of their divine soul, and their divine soul is them.

Read more on it, Mom. There are books out there that describe angels and spirits.

You need to think about things you want to ask me. I'm starting to wane on topics, and I don't know what you want to know. Get some more sleep.

Tomorrow.

Cindy's voice:

I think I can come up with questions. The problem is that I have so many, and I know that our time is short. I resolved to think of questions before our transcendental conversations so that I could be ready.

CHAPTER 14

MUSIC, LAUGHTER AND COLORS IN THE AFTERLIFE

Cindy's voice:

I asked for guidance from my divine self and spirit guide as well as Alec's, to allow words to flow onto these pages through my fingers, to convey what should be shared with the physical side. I hoped to hear from Alec more about the afterlife and get some answers to my many questions.

Alec's voice:

There is a soft but constant note that plays in the background here. It is a calming note. It is there, even underneath the music that plays, to remind us of the constancy of love and our eternal afterlife. You get so used to it being there that you don't hear it any longer, but you know it's there. I sometimes listen for it just to remind myself of its presence. No one told me what it was or why it plays. We all know that it's there, and that it won't disappear.

I wish I'd been receptive to music when I was on the physical side. There is so much music that has been written throughout the years. The celestial music that plays is soft and like something you might hear when you are getting a massage at one of those fancy spa places. But I like the intermittent brief melodies that play.

You were listening to some music yesterday that was like what we hear in the background. It was two alternating, soothing tones. The most soothing notes are 'C', 'E' or a 'G', and there is humming with voices, sort of like 'I am' with the vowel syllables drawn out. Very subtle, soft. As I said, sometimes a soprano voice sings, but not really with words, only notes.

I can listen to my own music if I want to. I conjure it up and it will play. I still like to listen to the music that I used to code or study by. Electric synthesizer, steady beat. I play this whenever I want, especially when I'm trying to concentrate on something. It helps me focus.

In concerts, all kinds of music can be heard. It's really fascinating because we all may show up wanting to hear different music. The musicians can sense that and start "playing" the music that touches everyone. It has a little of all the music that everyone wants to hear. I can hear what I want in the notes played, and others near me will hear what they want. We also share in what others around us wanted to hear, so it can be a very enriching experience. You can basically get what you want out of the experience. You can focus only on what you want to hear, or you can try different types of music so that you learn what you like and what doesn't resonate with you.

The concerts are only instrumental, or voices without words. As I've said before, words are not used here. I suppose it would be hard to use words because of all the different languages that souls have spoken over time and in different cultures. When we communicate, it's by vision and emotion.

Sometimes I hear the voice of a female angel singing. I stop and listen to really hear it. I think it might be when a soul becomes one with their divine self. It has some ceremony feel to it.

"Have you seen colors and patterns of the music that plays there?"

I don't see colors that flow to the rhythm and tones of the music, although there are beautiful colors here. Music calms me even here. It can be playing in the background, and I barely notice it until it goes silent. Then I really feel the silence until it starts back again. I would say I feel the music more than I 'see' it. My emotions rise and fall with it sometimes. At concerts, I feel the crescendo of the music inside of me. I never knew music could be so emotional.

"That's one of the reasons I loved playing classical music. The emotion of it helped me calm down. At the concerts, are musicians playing the instruments? Have you seen instruments playing on their own?"

All the instruments I've seen have musicians playing them, at least at the concerts I've attended. For the background music, I don't know if there are musicians playing or not. Instruments playing of their own accord is certainly something that seems possible here.

"Do you ever hear musical notes that are not heard here on the physical side? That our human ear can't tolerate or pick up?"

Yes, I have heard notes like that. Both high notes and low register notes. It's like we aren't restricted by human auditory limitations.

Have we talked about the bells? I suppose bells have always been symbolic of angels and heaven. Occasionally, we hear a bell ring. Like the bells that are played in church. Only one note, distant but clear.

"What does it signify?"

I am not certain because I am not there where they are ringing, but I sense it may be when a spirit becomes an angel. Remember at the end of that movie called *It's a Wonderful Life*, the little girl says, "Teacher says every time a bell rings, an angel gets their wings"?

When I'm not intensely learning, I told you I tend to explore or visit with family and ancestors. Sometimes I let myself go, being free to sense whatever may come. It's so freeing. I like to let that freedom absorb me sometimes. When I do that, I see and sense beauty that sometimes overwhelms me.

Our souls have so many manifestations that are in different learning cycles, and exploring so many different layers or dimensions of the afterlife, that it's a constant feeling of calm multi-tasking. It would have overwhelmed me in my physical life since multi-tasking was always a challenge. That's why I sometimes try to pause, and let go, and bathe in the wonder of it all. When I do, I am rewarded with that beauty and love.

I see love everywhere. It is all-consuming. A constancy for us but one that we never take for granted or get so used to that we don't notice anymore. It is part of our souls. And because of that, there is the total acceptance of every soul that I spoke of earlier. And that love spills over into everything in the afterlife.

The valleys and streams, the hills and oceans. There are trees and plants here too, often in different colors than what you see on earth. There are animals. The soul of cats, dogs, horses are the ones that are closest to us as souls, maybe because they were closest to us on the physical side. Other animals are in different dimensions than the ones we tend to frequent.

We don't interact that much with the animals, but they are there for us, loyal to us. Bucky and Lexi will be here for you when you arrive along with me, waiting to show you this realm.

Papa and I hung out together, and we were communicating about the holiday coming up and the family getting together. We miss our family on the physical side, but we know we will see all of you soon, some sooner than others. We are comforted and at peace with that because whatever duration of time it takes to be reunited, it is only a moment here. I hope you and Dad will be comforted too. The circle of life: mortals live, and they die. It is an experience to be enjoyed as much as you can during your physical lifetime.

You should get outdoors in nature more. Hike in the mountains, wander in the forests, wonder at the plants and birds. Get together with others and tell stories and laugh.

"Do you laugh in the afterlife, Alec?"

Yes, we "laugh". We "tell" jokes and find humor in many things. The awe of things is more compelling though, and Papa and I talk about that a lot. The awe of what God created, not only on earth. Earth is only a small part of it all. You will understand when you arrive here. That initial charge of knowledge is like a huge download of understanding about the connectedness of All Things.

Speaking of connectedness, sometimes I am a bird outside in the trees in the yard. I chirp or call, but you don't know I'm there. Be assured that I am. Whether I am in the birds or grass or trees or mountains, I am there with you always, wherever you are.

The beauty of a soul is that it can have many experiences at once. I can be with you, with Vera, with other family members and at the same time, learning many topics and exploring. It's amazing.

I have not sent you visions lately that would show you the extraordinary beauty of the afterlife. Not for several days, anyway. Let me try to give you a vision or two of the beauty here.

Do you see a distant view of hills and a stream running through it that leads to somewhere but gives the impression that 'somewhere' is forever? There are greens and rich warm browns and purples and yellows, overlaid with blue skies and soft clouds. The further away the mountains are, the darker they become. I send you mountain views because you love the mountains so much. You always say it's like you are 'home' when you are in the mountains of western North Carolina.

Another view of vast water. It could be a large lake, or it could be a bay. There are very subtle soft waves, gently caressing the shore, with a few rocks here and there. Let your mind open so you can see the colors. They are unlike colors on earth.

Soft lavenders on the shore, a bright light in the water's edge. Intense blue green water. The water extends into the horizon and continues outward on either side. Only the edge in front of you is visible. The lapping of the water gently against the lavenders is mesmerizing. I know you love the ocean too.

"Is the sky blue? Is grass green? Are the trees made of bark?"

Open your mind, Mom. Don't apply your earthly knowledge to what you might see here. You are thinking of the yellow brick road, aren't you, Mom?

"Yes! I am. How'd you know?"

I know what you think. And I clearly got that image. I haven't seen things like that, but that really doesn't mean much. I've only been here a short while.

There are trees and plants in specific views, but there are a lot of vines that grow quickly and spread everywhere. The vines have a soul, too. They are ancient, extending back as far as we can imagine. The vines extend into almost everything, but they aren't scary. Some painters have made them look scary, but they aren't.

I like to hang out with some of the animals sometimes. It is amazing to be able to sense their spirit and what guides them here and what drove them in their physical life. Most animals in their physical life are driven by food and water, and while some animals are feared because they are carnivorous, that's how they survive. The circle of life.

I wish you could sense the beauty of it all and how things are so connected. Our connection to All Things includes the animals and all growing things on the physical side. And in the afterlife, we know and understand all of those and how they are all connected and meant to be.

Survival of the fittest is true only to a certain extent. It is God's plan how All Things survive and die and become. It depends on where it is needed most in the connectivity of All Things.

I hunger for knowledge and understanding. I always feel love and acceptance but never tire of it and never, ever take it for granted. It consumes us all and allows us to be in this state of bliss.

"Are you there, Alec? Where in the room are you? I am not sensing you beside me, but rather, almost in me."

That is true Mom. I am with you, in you, and all around you.

Breathe, Mom. I know it's a lot to take in. But here you are, doing it. Be proud and don't let it overwhelm you. Let it bathe you with its light. And don't forget your vitamin C, Mom. Remember the medium said you were low on vitamin C. It was true, but it was also meant to get you outdoors in nature, even in the cold. I know you don't like the cold so much. I loved it.

Be present, Mom. Your mind is wandering to what you are planning to do today. Be here in our transcendental conversation with me.

"Sorry, Alec. It's what human minds do. I'm here. I can feel you around me and with me. It's amazing to sense you here."

Leave the writing for a moment. Come with me.

"I see a vastness ahead of me, but a being off to the right side, that I know intuitively is Alec, trying to pull me along. Splotches of green and orange are along the 'path'. Like an abstract painting or a child's fingerpainting."

We have a lot of those here.

"The path seems to go down and around."

That is what you sense because it is continuous and infinite, and that's how mortals can conceive of infinity, a circle that continues forever.

"I see a bear, a large black bear."

Be careful of them, Mom. On the physical side, they are dangerous, especially if a physical human interferes with their food or their cubs. If they come into the backyard and they look friendly, don't approach them. I know you want to.

Come along now, Mom.

"Trout. Water. A stream sparkling in the light. I wasn't aware of the light until now.

An orange sky. With the orange between clouds like edges across the sky. It is dawn.

Birds tweeting.

Where are we, Alec?"

It's a vision. Be present.

"A boat. A small boat, rowing. Fishing. Catching trout. Where is the bear?"

Don't worry about the bear, Mom. Just enjoy the view.

"Another view. At dawn still, but of ocean waters. Brighter sun. It is rising in the sky. Boats. Small fishing boats dot the water. A pier. A sea turtle. Am I seeing these things because these are some of my favorite things?"

"I'm seeing another view. This time a meadow. Birds at the edge, up in trees. The meadow is beautiful, with grasses swaying in the breeze. The dew on the grasses makes it look like tall stalks of green ice. A butterfly lands on a branch of the grass, then takes off again, beating wings gently in the air. The only sound is the sound of the breeze, very faintly rustling through the trees and the grasses. A fox hunts in the shadow of the high grass."

Nature, Mom. Get out in it. Enjoy it. Enjoy the peace of it.

Did you notice how the visions changed and transitioned from one to another?

"Yes, Alec. It all the sudden was something different."

That's what it's like in the afterlife. But multiplied by infinity. We have so many visions - of physical life, of the afterlife, of different universes. It sometimes transitions like I showed you, but more often, all those visions are seen at the same time.

"It's like you have an infinite number of trains of thought at the same time?" I asked.

Sort of. Only they don't get jumbled and there is sensing, not vision, in everything we are experiencing.

"A park with benches, swings, dogs."

Get out with your new puppy and play.

"OK, Alec. I will try. But we humans have to work, too."

"You're a consultant, Mom. Start scheduling time for you, and for you and Dad, to enjoy."

"I will, Alec."

I must go now. It's time. Dawn has come, and it's more difficult for me to communicate now.

Until tomorrow.

Cindy's voice:

I was thrilled that I could sense Alec in the room with me, and almost inside of me, during this transcendental conversation. I was not able to sense him right beside me before. It gave me comfort.

The views of heaven were fantastic to receive. It gave me such joy that he could send them to me and that I could receive them. I hope he will send me many more.

CHAPTER 15

PICK-UP FOR THE WEEKEND

Tom's voice:

There was no answer to the knock on the door of his apartment. I knocked harder. I banged and yelled for Alec with no response. I banged and yelled louder. I walked to the other side of the building to see if he was on his deck. Not there. My mind was spinning. Washington, D.C. all over again. I went to the apartment complex office and told them I suspected something was wrong. The apartment complex office wouldn't let me in and told me to call the police and request a wellness check.

The police arrived a half hour later and got the full story, then said that they could look around the outside of the door to his apartment for cause. Without cause, they cannot enter the property. I didn't know I needed to use the words 'wellness check'. All they could do was bang on the door. I'd already done that. I pleaded with the officer in charge. I told him I would sign a waiver, whatever it took, because I was convinced something was very wrong. I explained how this had happened before and that he could be unconscious, or worse. The officer made some calls.

The local sheriff and security for the apartment complex then showed up with a key and tried the lock. The door had two deadbolts. One could be opened from the outside, a second only from the inside. The inside deadbolt was engaged. Someone was in there and not responding to the loud banging and yelling.

After much pleading, the police agreed to treat the apartment as a crime scene so that they could enter. The fire department arrived and broke down the door.

I stood outside, breathing in fast, short, nervous breaths. Holding tears back behind the lump in my throat. I felt simultaneously numb and so nauseous that I thought I was about to be violently sick.

The police and firemen went in. The firemen came out only a few minutes later.

"Where is Alec?"

"He is gone, sir."

Gone? How could he be gone? Hoping against hope, I thought he meant Alec was not in the apartment.

"He is deceased, sir."

I went completely numb. My soul disconnected from my body. I watched myself talk with the fireman.

It was a blessing that I did not have to identify his body. I called Cindy, trying to keep myself together. I didn't know how I would be whole again.

"Is he in there?" she answered immediately.

"No. He's gone."

"What do you mean, he's gone? Where did he go?"

"Honey, he's deceased. Gone. He has passed."

I heard the long loud wail through the phone, like the howl of a wild animal in terrible pain.

The police did a thorough investigation of the crime scene and waited until arrangements could be made to remove Alec's body before I was allowed in to get Alec's traumatized cat. Then I drove the two hours home. Cindy begged me not to drive but to check into a hotel or go stay with friends. All I wanted was to be home, with my wife, and cry.

The local sheriff had summoned a chaplain from a local volunteer service and was with me for five hours during all of this. This was a gracious and welcome volunteer service for those going through such traumatic events.

Alec had been in recovery for nearly twenty months when he passed. We thought he was strong in his commitment not to use. Unfortunately, the last time we saw Alec, just three days before he passed, he was high. He adamantly denied it, of course. He always did. But we knew and it concerned and frustrated us greatly, which is why we were happy that he was planning to come home to visit that weekend.

Alexander Vitaly Girman, born near Kaliningrad, Russia on 6/21/1999 and adopted by us on 2/15/2000, died alone in his apartment sometime on 10/20/2021. I found him two days later. Our greatest fear, our worst nightmare, had become a reality.

ALEXANDER V. GIRMAN & CYNTHIA J. GIRMAN

CHAPTER 16

SPIRIT TEACHERS AND ANGELS

Cindy's voice:

It's much later today. I feel like I need to apologize to Alec's soul. I was tired and slept later. I pray that my divine self, my spirit guide and Alec's are not angry with me and will give me direction and let words flow to the page through me yet again.

"What is it like being a teacher there, Alec? It's a respected position and role, isn't it?"

Alec's voice:

Yes, it's a respected position, but it's not like a hierarchy you might find in your physical life. There are levels based on roles and the degree of growth and learning that a spirit has achieved, only so that others who need help can call on them for guidance and learning. It does not mean that they have more power or anything. It is not competitive at all. Everyone wants everyone else to be the best that they can.

Teaching guides have wisdom beyond other souls that haven't gotten through as much of the learning cycle. I was fortunate to get through a lot of learning, but I think it was because of objectivity. I had few preconceived notions about things here in the afterlife. When I started learning, I was able to absorb much of the material without emotion and accept it without many questions. Some souls have trouble with emotions and what they believed during their physical lifetime, and that makes it much harder for them to get through the concepts.

You should know that I was a spirit teacher guide long before this past physical life. I am sought by other souls who get stuck in their learning, or I can be dispatched to help those on the physical side. I say dispatched because either a mortal must call on me or the spirits of my higher self must ask me to help guide a specific human physical being. I try to guide them on their path through dreams, meditation, or signs.

"Can I call on you to help me, Alec? And in what ways can you help me?"

I cannot change the course of your life or anything. I can't interfere with your choices. But I can do things like help you find something or guide you along your path. You lost your air pods again, Mom. I can help with that. I can help guide you if you are lost and GPS isn't working for you. Or guide you to books you might enjoy or shows you might want to watch. Things like that. I cannot make someone well or keep them from dying. There are definite limits to what I can do.

"Can you guide me in what you can help me with?"

Unfortunately, no. You must ask for guidance. I cannot interfere. It's against God's law.

Souls can't give signs that are too obvious. We can't interfere with your lives. We can be in the cardinal song, or a butterfly or dragonfly that alights near you, or leave a feather. Or we can sometimes leave a dime or penny. The myths are true, those are signs. But there are others.

Did you know you can appeal to your spirit guide to help you find things? I think some people call on archangel Saint Michael. He is the highest archangel. Sometimes a spirit guide of a manifestation of a soul will answer to that name because they know it is meant for them, or Saint Michael will ask them to help. Saint Anthony is often who Saint Michael sends to help people find things that are lost.

"Can they help me find my airpods that have been missing for months?"

Yes, but you need to call on them specifically.

"I will do that Alec. What else can we call on our divine soul's spirits for?"

You can seek guidance from your higher self, but your higher self cannot act. Only the spirits do that, like your spirit guide, or your Master spirit, your guardian angels, and teaching spirits.

"How do you know which ones to call on? "

I can guide you to some books, Mom. They've been written. There are so many spirit guides. But your first call should be to your guardian angel and the spirit guide of your divine self. Next, you could call on your life guides or the spirit teachers guides for your divine self. If you're having problems with a specific project, you could call on creative guides or helper guides. If you need healing, there are healing guides, too.

"I am so grateful to connect with you and being able to share this experience with others."

It is an honor.

It is difficult to communicate with your spirit guides if your mind is not still. For example, for the months after my death, your spirit guide could likely not communicate with you because your grief was too deep for the spirit guide to get through to you. And even when you try to still your mind, sometimes you have a lot of clutter–thoughts about what you need to do and work projects. If you let those thoughts go and keep quieting your mind, you eventually will be able to communicate. It takes practice and you are only beginning to try. Once you still your mind, you can pray to your spirit guide and teacher spirits, like you pray to God.

Angels are not like what everyone thinks of on earth. They don't have wings but wear flowing garb to signify their status. The archangels have the highest status of angels, and they are regal. All of us aspire to be one and achieve understanding and light that will allow us to move closer to the archangels, then to the highest light and infinity of God. Messengers of God help Him by calling on angels and spirit guides to help in what is meant to be.

There is a lot of structure here in terms of angels. And then there are the divine soul spirits. It's a little confusing until you figure it out.

"Can you explain it to me, or is it too complicated for me to understand?"

I will try.

Angels are higher beings and there is a definite hierarchy in their roles in heaven. This is well documented in books on the subject, Mom. The archangels are the highest of the angels and the closest to God. There are many other levels of angels below the archangels that can be called upon for various things.

My divine soul consists of many soul lives and has many spirits. One spirit is my spirit guide. There is a Master spirit, and there are other spirits as well. There are teacher spirit guides at different levels, which is what my role is. I am at the intermediate teacher level, as I told you, so I help the more junior spirit teacher guides in their learning and teaching. There is also an advanced spirit teacher guide, which is my growth and learning level, and they help other spirit guides, as well as human beings on the physical side when they need it. Sometimes we are asked to help in situations where it is difficult for us to act. It is intense learning and will require fuller focus from me than the usual learning I have. Up until now, I have been responding to simpler requests. It's time now for me to take on more difficult ones.

"When do I call on my divine soul spirits and when do I call upon angels?"

It is hard to say, but you should call on your divine soul spirits to help for little day-to-day things and the angels for guidance in important choices and to depart divine wisdom.

"It sounds very similar. It seems like there is overlap between them."

Yes, there probably are some. That's the way it was designed, so that there are no gaps.

Mortals don't call on their divine soul spirits and the angels nearly enough. Some mortals do so daily, but others don't even know they exist. Human beings on the physical side have a long way to evolve.

Your higher self is you. And you are your higher self. You are one. You are living an experience that your higher soul believed was needed for it to evolve and grow.

"Which is it, Alec? Is it higher soul, higher self, or divine self?"

They are all intended to mean the same higher self that is you.

Your higher self cannot act on your behalf. But the spirits of your higher self can. That's who you should call on, like you have me to help you write this book.

My higher self was proud of me when I became a spirit teacher guide.

"But isn't your higher self you? So didn't your higher self also become a spirit teacher guide?"

In a sense, yes. But in another sense, no. There are many prior lives that make up my higher self, and not all of them are spirit teacher guides. My soul exists, even though it is part of my higher self. It is my soul that is a spirit teacher guide, and I've been a teacher guide for many lives.

"I hope you can help me find those air pods, Alec. It's the second set I've lost."

I know. You have a hard time keeping up with them. I think you need a bigger case or something.

"That's a good idea. One that will stick out of the seat pockets on a plane!"

I will help you find them. Give me time. They may not be where you think.

Teacher guides here also continue to learn. It's not like they stop learning when they become teacher guides. We have special layers in the wheel of learning, where only we can be. Teacher guides learn about what we can do as spirit teacher guides and how we can acquire more and more knowledge. We learn about the history of teachers. Some of the famous prophets achieved being teachers on earth, but not many. Many of the archangels were teachers once. Some of them were teachers or prophets on earth in their physical life. That is inspiring. We as teacher guides aspire to learn and grow as much as we can to become the best we can. That is a lot of learning, inner focus and forgiveness, both of myself and others. It will take a great deal of work, but there is plenty of time.

"So it's an infinite journey?"

In a sense, yes. But there is hope and real possibilities of becoming an angel. As a spirit teacher, I have a better shot than most. But again, it's not competitive, only aspirational. It gives us hope. And we all want to grow and become one with our divine spirit, and one with our higher beings.

It's not like the pressures of climbing the corporate ladder. It's not a reporting hierarchy with power, but rather a recognition of who spirits can call on if they need knowledge.

You must go now and start your workday. Tomorrow, make it earlier, Mom.

"I will, Alec."

Cindy's voice:

It's good to understand what spirit guides I can call on when I need help. Why did I always think it was up to me to solve all my own problems? Maybe this was a way to reduce my anxiety. I should start reaching out to my spirit guides. I was wishing for a menu of options so I could remember which ones to call on for what!

ALEXANDER V. GIRMAN & CYNTHIA J. GIRMAN

CHAPTER 17

LIGHT AND DARK

Cindy's voice:

It's dark outside, and early the way Alec likes. I pray to my higher self and to my spirit guide to help me and guide me in writing. I plea with Alec's higher self and spirit guide to let the words flow from Alec's soul to my fingers on the keys.

Today I am curious about Alec's role as a spirit teacher guide and whether it is an angel position or a spirit teacher guide. I start off with a question.

"Are you an angel teacher, Alec?"

Alec's voice:

No, I would need to be purer, and learn and grow a lot more to be an angel, especially a teacher angel. I am an intermediate teacher spirit.

Angels have been learning and becoming for a long 'time'. I know I said there is no 'time' here, but you can tell that they are much revered, full of knowledge and power from through the ages, because they are angels.

I teach other souls in the learning cycle. Angel teachers help human beings on the physical side. They work with the other angels and even the archangels. I don't know a lot about them yet. They have a special 'place' in the time-space continuum where they learn and communicate with each other.

They are many levels of angels, each with a different mission. They are all working with the archangels to preserve love and peace here and everywhere, even on the physical side.

You would have to communicate with angels more directly to learn more.

It is Thanksgiving tomorrow. I always thought that was a strange holiday, but it is good to have a day where everyone in America gives thanks and spends time with family. That should happen every day, though. You should be grateful daily for the privilege and experience of your physical life, your loved ones, and all the love and joy in your life.

I can sense that you are becoming less burdened with sadness and grief. I am happy that these transcendental conversations have helped you heal a little. I know you miss me, but you don't have to because now you really know that I am with you, all around you, and will always surround you until you arrive here. And then I will greet you and welcome you to eternal life. I can't wait to show you around and teach you. But that will come. Take time now to enjoy life, travel, spend time with friends and family, and live life to its fullest. Be healthy, go outdoors and walk every day with your new puppy.

I am here beside you, all around you. I think you sense me.

"Yes, Alec. I do. It's amazing."

Have I told you that all your relatives are very proud of you? Your grandmother, Mama Mac, shared that with me. She has a strong presence as a soul.

"She was always strong. I admired her greatly."

She knows that. And she is touched by the scholarship you and Dad established in her name to help students with their education, especially in epidemiology and nutrition. Papa, of course, has always been proud of you, and he misses all of you very much. Sometimes he says he feels like he didn't know you, Dad, Vera and me on the physical side.

"Maybe that's because of his dementia in his last few years?"

No, although that's a part of it. He wishes he'd spent more time with us and knew more about what went on with our family back in my high school years.

"It's hard to do that when we lived hours away from each other."

Yes, but he's glad you talk to Nana twice a week now. You both keep up with each other and he's happy about that. Of course, he misses the love of his life, but he is always with Nana. It's funny how he always calls Nana the love of his life. She truly was and still is the love of his life. He's still singing that Johnny Mathis song "Chances Are". He loved that song!

"Tell me more about that, Alec. You always mention families and I assume that includes spouses, even though they aren't blood relatives?"

Yes, usually souls are part of a family because of the genetic link with their children. But people without children or like ours, with adopted children, are still with their spouses.

It's not that you are with your family and not with anyone else. Remember that we are all connected with one another.

"Does your light essence grow as your soul grows in knowledge and experience?"

A little. There are smaller and larger orbs of light that reflect your soul, and it loosely corresponds to how much you've learned and what your role is. I am a spirit teacher guide, so my orb is a little bigger than other souls. And my aura color changes as I grow and learn. But there is no competition. It merely is.

Angels, even on the lowest rung of the ladder of angels, are more humanoid in your light essence and become more so as you get into the archangels. They are regal and beautiful to behold. The lower angels are more like the beginnings of human-like figures of light.

It's hard to describe, so I may not be communicating it exactly as it is. I'm doing my best.

As a teacher guide, I don't dwell on angels and status. I teach other souls how to become their true self, how to understand their true inner 'me'. This is necessary before they can become one with their higher self.

"What about evil and Satan? Lucifer? Did they or do they exist?"

There is always good and evil on the physical side. There must be both to provide some balance and to allow choices. It's the ying-yang. Mortals on the physical side also need to have choices in their lives. Evil very much exists in your world. But not here. At least we don't experience it in our dimensions. But that's only my experience. Perhaps if I was evil on the physical side, I would know those dimensions and those dimensions would be there in this realm. I don't know. The higher beings, including God, know only of goodness, acceptance and forgiveness. God is only pure and knows only love.

"Tell me about Joshua."

You went to three mediums, and they all brought up a 'J' name and one of them mentioned Joshua. Joshua can be spelled Jeshua, and it is the old Hebrew name for Jesus. We all aspire to have the knowledge and love and light of Jesus. He is the closest to God, as his son. Souls cannot be in the presence of God and Jesus because of the intensity of Their light. Souls must become pure to do that. But we all feel Their presence. We know They are there because They are part of us. All of us will strive for eternity to be one with Them.

"What should I know about the physical side you wish you'd known when you were physically alive?"

That's a hard question to answer because there are things I can't share. All that I have been telling you is what I want you to know. Experience, truly experience the beauty of earth and nature. Let go of your fears. Love. Live. Breathe.

… No really, breathe Mom. You forget to breathe sometimes when we're having these conversations.

Love. Live. Reflect that love in all you do. Joy is part of the actual word enjoy.

If you learn nothing else from our sessions, learn this: Life is not happening *to* you. Life is to be experienced *by* you. Don't sit back and think that what happens is beyond your control. It is not. There are so many decisions and choices you can make to change what is happening in your life. Grasp life. Don't let it control you. You control what you experience. Live life to your best ability every day. Pursue. Reach. Don't wait for things to happen. You are good about that with some things, but with others, you need to try harder.

You know I cannot interfere with your choices and your physical life. But know that you can reach out to us. There are spirit guides that can help you on the physical side if you ask. Learn to reach out.

You have always been hesitant to ask other people for help. You started doing that a little more after I passed. Keep doing it. People inherently want to help others. And you will help anyone else without question. It is a sign of strength, not weakness, to ask for help. And do more than donate money. Really actively help others if you can. It will bring you fulfillment.

"Can I ask the spirits questions? Can they guide me when I have choices?"

Yes, they can.

"How do I know it's the positive spirits and not some sort of negative or evil spirit?"

You will know. Like I know the makeup of mountains and streams. Of birds and butterflies. You know.

I must go now. It is dawn. Tomorrow is a holiday, and you will be with family. Be with them in love. I hope you can find a way to continue our sessions.

Cindy's voice:

Alec again has given me much to think about. I loved the part about life being something experienced *by* you, not something happening *to* you. All too often, I knew I was living my life day to day, reacting to whatever comes along, instead of taking control of my life and making it what I want it to be. Very good food for thought.

CHAPTER 18

THE STRUGGLES WERE REAL

Tom's voice:

Alec had been experimenting with drugs for years, but nothing like what we had found in D.C. When he was a sophomore in high school, we found a stash in his room. He had it stuffed into a large floor pillow where the seam had ripped. We had a long talk with him and restricted access to his laptop. We tried to stay calm because Alec didn't react well otherwise; he tended to shut down.

His sister Vera found prescription bottles of ours, a few pills of his ADHD medication, and a bottle of Z-Quil in his desk. While we were concerned, it wasn't a large amount, so we rationalized it away. Vera began to suspect that he was sneaking around more than we knew. We again had long discussions with him, reminding him he had a family history of substance use disorders. We knew addiction had a genetic component and ran in families. We had been told that his birthmother in Russia had been a heroin addict, so this had always been one of our biggest fears.

We described what happens when people become addicted. Cindy described someone she went to high school with whom, decades later, still wandered around begging for money for his next fix. We described the life that many addicts have and found videos showing the misery of addiction. It didn't seem to matter.

Less than a year after finding this stash and tossing it, we figured out that he might not be taking his ADHD medication every day, but rather saving and crushing them to snort instead. We couldn't prove it, but pills seemed to be missing from the bottles in the kitchen cabinet, and we found rolled up dollar bills in his desk. He was a junior in high school. Even with us witnessing him take his medication every day, he started palming it in his hand for later. This was simply not working. We tapered him off and canceled the prescription.

When he was a junior, we left Alec studying for the SATs at home one Sunday in spring, and when we got home, he was not downstairs where we'd left him. I went upstairs, and he was lying on the bed asleep. That was unusual because he never took naps. We tried to rouse him, but he was sleeping hard. Then we started to get panicked because he wasn't waking up.

Having an unlocked liquor cabinet in the hallway outside of the office where he studied was too much temptation for him. This surprised us because Alec had never shown any interest whatsoever in alcohol. Usually Alec lied about things like this, even if it was obvious and we knew he was lying. We had always told him it was worse if he lied, but he would continue the lie once he started it, even if it was clearly not true. We always thought that the lies were part of his Asperger's syndrome. When we found Alec that Sunday passed out on the bed, he started immediately lying and saying he hadn't touched anything. However, he had been so inebriated that he had left a chat open on the computer. It was clear in black and white text that he'd sent to a friend, "I'm drunker than I've ever been." That one he couldn't deny.

Academically, Alec showed little interest in humanities subjects, and much more interest in science and math. As a high school freshman, he chose the information technology (IT) track, and he excelled in those classes and math and science, but much less so in other subjects. In the winter of tenth grade, his grades plummeted. He struggled to track his assignments, especially in AP classes, but he pushed his way through. We hired an academic coach. He started his junior year strong and was taking a heavy load of AP and Honors classes. During winter break, his teachers informed us he was missing a very large number of assignments in all his classes, despite coaching and close monitoring. His organization and tracking skills were poor due to executive function deficits from Asperger's, but he was smart and capable in the content of his classes. Nevertheless, a full load with AP and honors classes and extensive assignments were simply too much. We changed coaches; it did little good. We started checking every day what assignments were due because the school's online tracking system was never up to date. We requested 504 accommodations verbally in Jan 2016. A Section 504 Accommodation Plan provides a student who has an identified disability and/or impairment (like Asperger's or ADHD) with accommodations that will help ensure his/her academic success and access to learning. Unfortunately, the school did nothing. Alec's psychologist encouraged us to request 504 accommodations formally in writing. We finally set a meeting up in April 2016, when the school year was almost over. At the time, we asked about an IEP (Individual Education Plan) which would include further specialized services, but the school claimed it wasn't needed and suggested trying the 504 first.

Depending on the individual teacher, the 504 accommodations for Alec were generally not acknowledged and poorly administered, with some teachers even making remarks like 'he should be able to do this work as a junior'. He struggled in eleventh grade; in fact, he barely passed. In frustration, we asked the psychologist if it could be more than ADHD, specifically Aspergers, and he was finally diagnosed.

Alec proved he could do well in an AP humanities class online the summer after his junior year, primarily because it was very structured and organized. Alec's biggest issue was not being able to track a lot of assignments without a central mechanism in place.

Before his senior year started, we requested in writing an IEP meeting. The meeting was held, but an IEP was denied. More frustration with the school bureaucracy. We then met to look at revising 504 accommodations. Given the autism diagnosis, an autism caseworker was assigned to him to meet with him and follow-up with his teachers every week. This sounded like it would really help, and we were relieved.

The school year started well, and the caseworker met with Alec routinely. However, in the fall, meetings became sporadic and irregular, and things spun out of control with Alec falling way behind. It took legal counsel to get the accommodations enforced to a point where Alec could track his assignments. We were truly grateful for our niece, who taught English as a second language in secondary education in a different state, for all the advice she gave us throughout these years. Alec worked hard throughout his senior year and was able to graduate with a 2.9 grade point average. His technology and science classes saved him.

Soon after classes were over, Alec started part-time work at an office supply store. Because of his grades, he didn't get into any of the colleges to which he'd applied. He decided to work and go to the community technical college in IT with the hope of transferring into a college with a good IT curriculum. As he took classes and worked, we clung to the idea that he was doing better, until one day, he came home after the evening shift and walked by us in the den. The unique skunk odor of marijuana almost knocked Cindy over.

Cindy said, "Whoa, whoa, whoa, what you got there, bud?"

He said, "Nothing". I then smelled it, too. We asked him to show us the 'nothing' in his bookbag and there was his stash. He said that he had purchased odor-containing canisters online. We told him they didn't work!

"Where are the things you are buying online being shipped to, Alec?"

Oops, that was a slip. His face fell when he heard the question.

He had to admit that he had a post office box, so off we went to empty it and cancel it. Of course, he could just open another one. He had access to the car that he shared with his sister, and we couldn't follow him around all day.

Another day we came home from shopping, and Alec had left for work at the office supply store. We heard the cat meowing, but we couldn't find him. We searched the entire house but no cat. We went outside, thinking maybe he had slipped through the door when someone opened it. No cat in the bushes either. The meowing got louder though, and we finally figured out that it was coming from the attic crawlspace off the recreation room above the garage. In there, we found the cat and a lighter and bong, along with a bag of pot. Again we talked to Alec. He tried to deny it, but he was the only one home when we left and the cat was never locked up anywhere in the house, much less in a crawlspace.

We took him to sessions with a substance abuse counselor at Duke University. Alec hated those sessions, but he went without complaining. He knew he had been caught, so he followed through with the consequences. It seemed like he just said what he thought everyone wanted to hear in those sessions. Whether they helped at all was unclear.

Alec's sister Vera graduated from high school a year after Alec did, and we put the house up for sale to move to the beach, which had been our plan for years. Alec was able to get a job at the office supply store near there. Vera was heading to college for the next four years. We thought Alec would investigate transferring his credits to a community college nearby, but he had other plans. He started looking for computer coding (programming) jobs.

As Alec started becoming bored with the office supply store job, we started seeing signs of the erratic behavior we noted when he was in high school. He was starting to use Kratom, which was essentially a plant-based opioid. One day, just walking into Alec's room to see how he was doing, I saw what looked like white crystalline flakes on the top of his dresser. Not much, but enough to cause major concerns. This prompted drug testing and, even though the results were positive, he denied using anything. We were able to get a referral from his counselor in Durham that he saw a few years back and Alec started counseling again in Wilmington, North Carolina. We hoped against hope that the sessions would help.

CHAPTER 19

SOULS ALL AROUND

Cindy's voice:

A dark and dreary morning, I pray to the spirit guide and teacher spirits of Alec's and my own divine soul to give me direction and help me with words to share with the physical world. This morning I am prepared with several questions in case Alec is not prolific.

Alec's voice:

There are so many dimensions in the afterlife, it is hard for human beings to comprehend, but here's an attempt to try to explain.

Imagine a sphere and imagine north and south, east and west, but also inward and outward. You can comprehend that easily. But there are an infinite number of dimensions beyond those you can envision in your mind. We gain that understanding when we first enter this realm, and it is what we know as connectedness. This is how we connect with all there is.

When you become a soul, you will understand, and I will be there with you, as will Papa and all your relatives and ancestors. You will experience, you will know, and you will understand. You will be connected to all.

We don't really have sounds other than the music I described and bells ringing in the distance occasionally. The tone that I described to you plays constantly, and sometimes a melody will break out. There are times when choirs sing not so much words but harmonized notes that sound like "I AM", and melodies. Sometimes a single voice in soprano or alto can be heard. Unless I am at a concert, the music sounds as if it's in the background of a movie, soft and distant.

You were always afraid of heights and falling, weren't you? We don't have falling here. There is no notion of it. We are in all and are being in all. With the connectedness that is in you, there is total acceptance, love, and support. There is no falling and there is no failing.

"What about soaring? When you think about something or somewhere, is there a sensation of flying or soaring to whatever is in your mind?"

When you think yourself there, you then are there. There is no flight or flying. Human beings tend to think of heaven as above, up in the sky somewhere. It is everywhere. It is not one place. It is above and below and beside and inside. It is all around. Heaven is not a place. It is all around. It just is.

When I think of you, I am all around you. When my soul thinks of Vera, I am all around her, too. Vera is happy except for having to go back to work today. She is very tired. She enjoyed camping.

When you finally connect with your soul fully, you will understand about the connectedness.

"After you pass to the spiritual realm, when do you connect with your divine soul?"

You must pass through the initial stages of death and passing, then you will become one with your divine soul after gaining as much learning as you can about your experience on the physical side. It is almost as if you never left because your divine soul is with you on the physical side and as soon as you pass, you recognize your divine self within you again.

"Which spirits and angels do I ask for help with physical pain? Can any help me?"

As you get older, you will have conditions that are simply signs of the aging of your physical body. There is not a lot that can be done about arthritis and other aging of your physical body, unless you can raise the vibrational level of your body cells. The way to do that is to forgive yourself, think of others before yourself, forgive, accept, and love others.

As I said earlier, we are on a higher vibrational level than human beings. Pain is an experience of mortals that you should be able to rise above. You should start meditating. It should help. And call on healing guides, some of which live on earth.

It all works out, Mom. Do not fear death. On the contrary. Enjoy your physical life. Be present in it. Do things that make you happy. Travel and see the beauty. Your time for the spiritual world will come and you will not be able to go back and take the detour or trip or do other things that you didn't get to do.

"We all were thinking of you over the holiday, Alec."

I know. I can sense that. It calls me in. Especially when you are all missing me at the same time.

Do you see what looks like a very large sun rising over the horizon in your mind?

"Yes, Alec, I do. The light of it outshines everything so that the horizon and sky are muted in color."

That is not your sun. It is a sun in another universe. Much bigger than your sun compared to the planets in its solar system. We have different universes here to discover and understand. I can be in multiple universes simultaneously. Have you seen paintings of a single soul with identical shadows going in a circle around it? That is the painter's depiction of the infinite number of dimensions that a soul has. The circle is because the number is infinite; the shadows are because of the dimensions of the original soul.

"But you, as a soul, are also part of your divine soul?"

Yes, that's how it is. We are all connected.

Your physical life is pre-destined in a way. You will have choices, but much of your life is known to us because we know that dimension. The past, the present and the future are all dimensions. It's hard to describe.

I must go. We can have another session tomorrow.

Cindy's voice:

Seeing a sun from a different universe was mind-boggling. What else is out there beyond what mankind can see, even with their most powerful telescopes? Alec says our physical life is predestined in many ways, but that we have choices. That's hard to understand. When Alec talked about the life review, he said that after passing, a spirit could evaluate every choice they'd ever made and see what would have transpired if they had made different choices. I wondered if that was what he meant by our lives being predestined, because all the choices were known and finite. How many choices would that be, for how many mortal physical lives? My head hurts now.

CHAPTER 20

WHAT MORTALS NEED TO KNOW

Cindy's voice:

In the dark before dawn, I send up prayers to my own and Alec's guiding and spirit teacher guides to help me write the words.

There is something that is barely beyond my consciousness. Like when you can't remember something, but it feels like it's on the tip of your tongue. Then I see a classic picture of Jesus in his white garb with a brown sash.

Alec's voice:

Jesus is who we all aspire to be in spirit. He is the model of goodness and love and is closest to God. He is the only one who has become One with God. He is All Things.

"What about Abraham? And other famous prophets? And those from the bible? The disciples? John, Peter, Paul, Matthew, Luke? Adam and Eve?"

They are all higher beings.

"Is this simply a fragment of what I learned as a child in Sunday School and grew up to believe, Alec? Or is it real?"

I don't know if different souls see different higher beings based on their prior beliefs on the physical side. All I know is what I sense, what I feel, and the emotion that it brings. It's entirely possible that in different dimensions that I have not tapped into, there are different higher beings. But I do know that God is the Highest Being and Creator of All Things. People from other religions may have different names for the Highest Being, instead of God. His presence is magnanimous, all-encompassing, glorious and undisputable. It is a power that all of us feel. He instills love and forgiveness and acceptance beyond description. That love is all we need. He is All.

"It seems there is a hierarchy of higher beings, archangels, angels, and spirits of divine souls. Do any souls get greedy and try to move up the hierarchy faster than they should, like in the corporate world on the physical side?"

It is not competitive at all. It is not a reporting hierarchy, like in the corporate business world. It is simply a matter of respect for elders and higher beings who have learned and grown more in their pursuit of knowledge. We all accept and love each other. Every soul wants the best for every other soul. It is God's way.

"Oh, if only it could be that way here on earth on the physical side…"

It's worth aspiring to, but it's unlikely to happen in your physical lifetime. God created the mortal experience such that human beings would have choices. Remember the forbidden fruit? Human beings have choices so that they have free will and can choose how to live and experience their lives. That is how we all learn, as humans and as their divine souls.

Imagine what life would be like without choice. You would soon learn that you have no choice and life would become predictable and boring, even depressing, and likely demotivating. Certainly, it would be less enjoyable.

There are things I would like to see you do in the next year, but of course, you have a choice whether to do them or not. I'd like to see you start meditating every morning before you do anything else. Clear your mind and let in only positive thoughts. This will bring mindfulness, reduce your anxieties, and help you make clear decisions. It will also make you more receptive to communication from the afterlife. List and acknowledge your fears, then let go of them. Consider a few more books on awakening your soul and self-love, and then a retreat to help you find your true inner self. That will bring you love and peace and relieve a lot of your anxieties.

Dad could benefit from similar activities. I think everyone could benefit from starting their morning with some quiet mindfulness.

Reestablish your connection to your goals and your true inner self.

"You have suggestions for my immediate future. What about long-term?"

That is your choice, but I would love to see you take charge of your life and live it the way you want to, rather than letting it happen to you. Wake up every morning and think about what you'd like to do that day. Be mindful. Plan day trips and explore around you. There is so much beauty to see. Travel to enjoy nature and see the world. Remember the little slips of paper you created when you retired, that listed all the things you'd like to do on days during retirement? Start drawing them out and doing them. Maybe Dad should create some of those, too.

And give. Give from the heart and out of love. Help others who are not as fortunate as you. Pursue collaborating on research into substance use disorders. It could help so many people.

"What do you want me to tell the physical side, Alec? What is the most important thing to let us all know?"

Human beings on the physical side need to understand that there is an afterlife, and that their soul will experience an overwhelming love and acceptance that it is so blissful. They need not fear death so much, because no one dies. Their soul will live on in another dimension, and they will be filled with love beyond human comprehension. It is beautiful, it is blissful, and never to be feared. That's not to say that anyone should accelerate their physical death. Only that they should not fear it. All human lives have a purpose, and they need to complete that journey and learn from that experience.

I can't possibly describe this feeling of total acceptance and the depth and overwhelming bliss of the love we feel. It fills us completely. It is all we need. Love is the secret. The most important feeling. If you have love and are loved, nothing else matters. If you love completely, there are no hard feelings to contend with. The physical world needs so much more love.

"How could that happen? How could we instill more love here on earth? This is a time when there is so much hate on earth. So much that is contentious among factions of physical humans. What can we do to change that?"

It will take many physical humans. It is not something one mortal being can do. Although the right human being in the right position of power could help. You know politics is interesting, but much of it is about greed. And not only on one side. On both sides. They are not nearly as far apart as everyone thinks, at least about most things. Politics, money and power don't exist as concepts in heaven.

Politics was never my favorite topic anyway, and it doesn't matter here. Human beings have choices they can make to help change things, but that's their decision.

"Can spirit guides help influence who is named to office?"

No, that is beyond what we can do. We can help guide voters if they ask, though. But they need to ask from their own volition. You are not meant to influence politics as your life purpose, other than voting. You have other things that you are meant to do.

"Like what, Alec? Can you share with me what I'm meant to do?"

You have already been looking into research for more effective treatments for substance use disorders. You could have such a strong impact on availability of an affordable treatment for addiction that actually works, if you pursue it. So many people need it.

"I understand, Alec. I'm meeting with professors this week that are experts in substance abuse disorders, studies of psychotherapeutic approaches and this technology. They are very interested in this approach."

Do it. Involve your peers to help. People want to help. It's their nature. And the help they give should be done out of love.

You worry a lot, Mom. Try to relax and take care of you. Take ten minutes every morning to clear your mind. That's why they call it mindfulness.

"I am trying to get into the habit of meditating every morning. It's hard to do consistently, because as soon as I wake up, I'm on my phone, then feel like I should be starting work. But I know it would help calm and focus me in the morning before I do those things. Are you with Vera as she flies from Florida?"

I am always with her, as I am with you. Remember how I used to love flight simulators and landing planes at various airports? I am still fascinated by them, but I understand a lot more about the science of how planes fly now. And about other ways of transport that mortal physical beings haven't yet discovered. Someday, maybe mortals will evolve to not rely on fuel and the effects it has on their planet.

Dawn is here. The beauty of the sun is right on the other side of the mountains, not yet seen, but its light spreads a magnificent orange tinge above the mountains. Enjoy it if you can.

I am teaching soon. It's always a pleasure to write with you, Mom.

"And such a pleasure for me, Alec. I love you and miss you so much."

I know. But I am always here with you. And we can continue writing tomorrow.

Cindy's voice:

Alec was giving me excellent advice again, to take charge of my life and live it the way I want to, rather than letting it happen to me. Life isn't happening to me, but rather I am experiencing life and I have a choice every minute of every day to make it what I want, not to react to it.

If there was anything holding me back from pursuing collaboration and better research on effective treatments for addiction, it no longer was. I resolved to pursue it as best I could. Alec was right. So many people could be helped. There was an opioid crisis before the pandemic. With the isolation and frustrations of the shutdown with Covid-19, it was at terrifying heights.

CHAPTER 21

INTERNSHIP

Tom's voice:

T hrough a good friend and colleague of ours, Alec landed a paid internship at a start-up company in artificial intelligence (AI). It was a dream job for him because he would finally be paid to do what he loved, coding. He was excited to move to Washington, D.C. and we found a tiny studio apartment for him rather quickly. It was in a great location near Dupont Circle, close to the metro and an easy walk to work. He was ecstatic to have his own place, despite the tiny size. He said, "I don't need any more space. A bed, bath and a microwave and refrigerator. It's all I need."

I drove him up and helped him move his meager belongings in. One of the few times he let us take his photo was when he was packed up and heading out to move into his apartment in D.C. Alec hated having his picture taken. He started his internship a day later.

The first few months living in D.C., Alec was good about calling home and chatting, letting us know what he was up to. At first, he was excited to be exploring the city and riding the metro all over different parts of it. He loved the electric scooters that you could rent by the hour. He was walking a lot, and it was healthy for him, we thought.

At Thanksgiving, we bought Alec a train ticket to Roanoke, VA to visit family and have the family dinner with us. He missed the train.

Then he missed the next one because he went home and didn't make it back in time. He then missed yet another one. It was awfully fishy.

We got him a flight, and he missed the flight. Then he got a flight rerouted through Charlotte. He boarded in Charlotte for Roanoke, but when they started to land, they had to divert back to Charlotte because of high winds. He spent the night in the airport. Finally, he got a flight out the next morning and made it to Roanoke airport, and we all breathed a sigh of relief.

It was a shock to see him coming out of the airport terminal. I almost didn't recognize him and had to look twice. His head was bent down in an awkward, unnatural position.

"Alec, what's wrong with your neck?" Cindy asked. "Are you ok? What happened?"

"I don't know. I can't lift it up straight. It hurts if I do," Alec said.

"How long has it been like that?" I wondered.

"I don't know. A few weeks?" Alec guessed.

"Have you gone to the doctor?"

"No."

In addition, Alec arrived with no bags. "Where's your bag, Alec?" Cindy asked.

"Oh, I left it somewhere," Alec mumbled.

"What do you mean, you left it somewhere? You don't know where?" I asked.

"No, I can't remember where. I had it in the airport, but I don't remember where I left it." he claimed.

All of this added to the burden of worry we were already carrying like a two-ton weight.

The bent neck was so pronounced and worrisome that we took him to an emergency room in Roanoke. They diagnosed it as "Tech Neck", caused by prolonged and repetitive looking down at a phone or other screen for too long.

I couldn't help but wonder if it also couldn't be caused by sleeping in a funny position, especially if passed out.

A few weeks after Thanksgiving and five months after Alec started the internship, my wife was in D.C. on business. She went by Alec's apartment to take him to dinner. He knew she was coming and had attempted his version of 'cleaning a bit', but the apartment was a wreck. Cindy looked through his bookbag that was sitting open on the bed and again found a lot of pot. She wasn't sure what to do because it was becoming legal in so many states. So she put it off until after dinner.

They had a nice dinner and talked a lot. Alec was enjoying his work. He talked about the project he was working on in high-level terms. It sounded like he was having fun. But he didn't seem challenged in his job. It was more data gathering than coding. He was coding at night for fun and intellectual stimulation.

After dinner, Cindy and Alec spent several hours cleaning his apartment. Alec grumbled as he scrubbed the tub and swept the floors. Then Cindy asked him to take all the pot to the dumpster and throw it out.

Christmas came, and Alec took the train to Roanoke. This time, he didn't miss it.

We took him through a fast-food drive-through for a cheeseburger and fries to take back to Cindy's mother's house. Cindy and I, as well as her sister and husband, were all standing around talking to him and watching him eat. Maybe that made him nervous, but we all noticed his hands shaking, which wasn't a good sign. Of course, he lied when we asked about it. Alec went back to D.C., and we headed to our home in North Carolina, wondering if he was using and how much.

CHAPTER 22

VIBRATIONS AND SHADOWS

Cindy's voice:

It's 4:00 am and very quiet as I sit down at the keyboard. The monitor is bright. I pray to the spirit guide of my own divine self and of Alec's, to guide my fingers and help me tell a story worth sharing on the physical side. My guardian angel is hopefully with me, guiding me, as always.

Alec's voice:

This is a good time for me, Mom; this early, before all the distractions of the day begin. Even spirits like mine get distracted, not only human beings.

You are near the ocean now. The ocean is so calming, with the rhythmic waves. I have seen large bodies of water here that are calm against the shore. Very small waves, if any. The water is a beautiful blue, though. Sort of like the ads you see for exotic destinations, but even richer.

"Alec, is Papa OK? When he did the life review, did he have to go through all the horrors of World War II again?"

Yes, he did. He said that it was harrowing. But that's all done now, and he is in his blissful loving state. He has finally forgiven himself. Even though he was following mandatory orders, he always felt so terrible about the things he was forced to do as a gunner in the Air Force. He is loved and gives love. He's ok, Mom.

"That's interesting, Alec."

It's all amazing, Mom. It's so cool here. I can't wait to show you around.

"You mentioned you meditate and pray and that's how you rest sometimes. Tell me about meditating, Alec, because you were never really into that here on the physical side."

No, I wasn't. It really is a part of being a spirit. Meditation is how we reconnect with All Things, understand our connectedness to our true selves and divine soul. And truly feel our connection with God. It is something I do often, and that I teach others to do.

It's comparable to how physical humans meditate. On the physical side, meditation is about clearing the mind or at least quieting it, letting it be calm. On the spiritual side, it is not clearing the mind so much as settling into a single dimension or vibration so that you can focus on the connections.

"How do you settle into a single dimension, Alec? And is that how spirits visit the physical side? They settle into a single dimension that corresponds to the mortal physical being frequency or vibration?"

Yes, Mom! You are getting it! That's exactly right. Settling into that single dimension that corresponds to the vibrations of the human physical side is not easy, though.

"What is hard about it?"

We have so many vibrations that correspond to many, many dimensions. It is difficult to distill ourselves down to one when we are experiencing so much in so many different dimensions simultaneously.

"Is that because there are so many parts of your spirit that are in the different dimensions, like with different physical human beings or other souls, and doing different activities?"

Exactly, Mom. You're learning!

"Are you here with me, Alec?"

Yes, I am with you. I am also with Dad and Vera. And in many dimensions, doing different things. But I am always with you, Mom. If you need me, simply talk to me.

"I will from now on, Alec. It is such a comfort knowing you are right here with me."

It is love. I know that now. I always resisted hugs and closeness while on the physical side. It was part of my Asperger's. But I will give you a big 'hug' when you come home. Well, to the extent that spirits can hug.

"I suppose it is a little awkward if you can't touch."

But we can bond together. That's our hug. We connect and are continually connected.

"I asked yesterday if you saw shadows in the afterlife."

We don't really see shadows because, as spirits, we are energy and light. So wherever we go, there is light. If we bond with other spirits, we have more light. And the more we grow and learn and the purer we become, the more we absorb light. The light, in general, is in varying shades, like right before dawn, all the way through the peak of the day and then sunset. The light gets much brighter when you are closer to higher beings, even archangels, but especially Jesus and God. That light is extraordinarily intense, and you need to be purified to be in Their presence.

Beyond our light, in some places in the universes, there are shadows and darkness. Not in an evil sense, but as part of the galaxy structures with suns. I see few shadows where I spend most of my time, but there are some occasionally, in very specific shades of light. And like I said earlier, there is a dark place that we avoid. Where I am in the learning center, there are no shadows.

"How do you become purer, Alec?"

By studying, learning, and especially loving and forgiveness. Kindness. Teaching. All the things I am doing. But it takes a lot. As I've said many times, only Jesus has become one with God.

"Do you ever become one with all? I read somewhere that after much learning, a soul can become one with the universe and all that there is."

We are connected to everything, and everything is connected to us. I think what you mean is that a soul can become absorbed by the universe. But I have a mission and function to perform as a spirit teacher guide. I will become more and more connected to everything, but I won't become absorbed by the universe until I have fulfilled that role and am no longer needed. I hope then I can advance even further toward the higher beings, but it is not competitive. I will be in bliss whether I do that or not.

"I am so proud of you, son."

I know, Mom. I wish you could have known this 'me' while I was there on the physical side. But soon enough, you will know me here.

"Do you have any messages for me? Anything I should watch out for?"

Just be careful, Mom. You need to start exercising more and get outside. Take the puppy for walks. He loves that. And it will help you with your health and with your mindfulness.

You should get some sleep. You seem tired.

"I'm fine. It takes a lot out of me, these transcendental conversations early in the morning. It's emotional."

Until the next time.

Cindy's voice:

I thought about how much I wished I could hug Alec right now. When I see him again, we won't be able to hug, but it sounded like connecting with another spirit is very special. Someday I will understand.

CHAPTER 23

CONNECTING SOULS

Cindy's voice:

Early one morning in December, as Alec likes it, I plea to my own and Alec's spirit guides and guardian angels to guide me and help the words flow to give the message to the physical world that they wish to convey.

"Do you miss earthly things like your cat Chico?"

Alec's voice:

I do. But I know I will see him soon. Not soon in your time. But a very short while in the afterlife. Infinity strips time away. But we remember time from our physical life. I remember that time was hard for me to track even on earth.

"What else do you miss here on the physical side?"

I think I told you we miss food. The whole act of sitting down to a meal and eating with family or friends. Sometimes I think about a cheeseburger or steak dinner, and definitely chocolate cake and ice cream! But it's not a craving or a negative feeling.

I miss the sensations, like touch. Believe it or not! I was sensitive to touch and certain textures while on the physical side. But we don't have touch here, we are energy and light. We also don't have smell so much, only in memories. But we do have vision and emotion.

I have told you about the incredible sense of bliss that we are in perpetually. That bliss is also sensual. Like the feeling you have building up when you have sex. That feeling of desire mixed in with release. It is total bliss. Love and sensuality. But the sensuality is not a longing, it is a part of your true inner self. Mortal beings are too hung up on sexuality.

"I see hills in pastel colors, Alec."

Yes, I know you like mountains, so I want to share some of the scenery here that I think you would like. The colors are remarkable. Sometimes soft and pastel, sometimes vivid and bold. But not stark. Always pleasant.

"Can you tell me what our universe is like? What about other universes?"

It's amazing to see. The universe is so vast, and mankind has only seen a very small part of it. The planets in your solar system are portrayed in photos from satellites, but I have seen the distant planets much closer than the satellite views. They are beautiful in their own way, but none of them are earth-like. It's funny that mortals keep trying to find a planet like theirs. They should try to find a planet that doesn't need the resources that they are depleting! But then they would have to adapt, and mortals, as physical beings, don't like change.

There are other universes, Mom. And planets with life. Not human life, but intelligent life. Planets that have evolved over millions and millions of years. I can see the evolution because I can see past, present and future dimensions. The intelligent inhabitants on these planets take better care of their home and the resources of their planet. Earth will not exist one day because mortals haven't paid attention to its resources. They are rapidly destroying their planet.

Exploring the universes is exciting, but it can be lonely too. After a while, I usually want to be back where most of the spirits are and be with my soul groups. Remember, though, that I can stay there and only one part of me goes to another dimension.

It takes a lot to be fully present with you. Especially the transcendental conversations because I need to translate into words and when you don't use words often, it becomes harder to remember them.

I have been teaching more often. That is draining sometimes. It takes a lot to generate the visions that are recorded for learning. But I truly enjoy doing it. I have always enjoyed teaching. Maybe because I've always enjoyed learning.

"You were a very inquisitive child, and you turned into a curious man. You were always an excellent teacher with a strong curiosity about science and technology."

Yes, and I think that helped me here to understand a lot about the way things work and are connected, and the different dimensions that we can exist on.

"What do you love most about the afterlife, Alec?"

First and foremost, the total bliss of love and acceptance is what I love most about the afterlife. And the freedom from the physical body constraints. It's so incredible. You can't imagine how free you will feel when you don't have physical ailments and your physical limitations, keeping you from feeling the strong emotions and keeping you from traveling through time and space in multiple dimensions. It's amazing.

"What happens when you are first without your body? Is it like riding a bicycle for the first time? Do you have to find the rhythm of being back in the spiritual realm or something?"

I described what I felt when I first arrived in the afterlife. When you receive that initial download of knowledge, you know how things work and how everything is connected, including your soul. You think of something or somewhere, and then you are there. After the first time, I knew how to do it. But the family and my ancestors all helped me understand how things work, too. They connected with me immediately, and I knew. You feel relief when you connect with family, because you know them and love them, and you know they love you. Total acceptance and love.

"What about family members that a spirit didn't get along with on the physical side? What if you die and are met by those family members? Is all forgiven?"

All is forgiven and you have only love for one another.

"It's amazing, Alec. And I'm seeing hills again, with a full moon lighting a path through them. It may be a river, I'm not sure."

Yep, it is amazing. I'm glad you like the scenes I sent you. I try to send you images you will like. I know you like art too. That helps a lot, because so many scenes here look like an artist painted them.

"Why do I see black figures on the hills, or below and all around the hills?"

It's merely a portrayal of souls. It's not what we usually see, but you wouldn't be able to see them with your naked eye against those pastel hills if they were white light. They aren't black.

"I see a picture of Jesus, praying and light in front of him. He's wearing a robe. It's a classic picture that we've seen a lot in our lifetime here on the physical side, in religious materials."

Yes, I give you that so I can try to explain. You see the light that He is praying in front of. He is in awe of the light that bathes Him. The light is God's light, and Jesus is one with God now. Mankind portrayed Him this way, but He is an extraordinarily intense light that is one with God. We often see visions of the One God, but also separate and beside God. All of us aspire to be one with God.

"That is so lovely, Alec, and consistent with what many believe, no matter what their faith or religion."

Yes, it is consistent, and it is All. It is the Be of All. The ultimate love and good, acceptance and forgiveness. The highest knowing.

We will continue again. More often, Mom. It's been a week, and I can only do this a little while longer.

"I love you, Alec. One of my biggest fears right now is losing touch with you, now that I have been connected through these transcendental conversations. I don't want to lose you yet again."

You won't lose me. I am always with you. All you need to do is call on me. Talk to me. I am there. But I won't be able to help you write for much longer.

"Will you talk to me? Will I hear words from you?"

You may not hear words, but I will try to convey emotions, visions. It's how we communicate here. It's getting harder for me to communicate with words. But I will be there, Mom. And I will greet you when you come home.

Until next time that we write.

Cindy's voice:

What a reassurance that all my family and friends who have passed are there with me, and that I can call on them. It gives me strength, calms me and, most of all, gives me hope. I will be with all of them someday.

Alec keeps saying that his time is running out for these transcendental conversations. I don't know how long he will be able to continue them, but I will try again tomorrow. Not being able to reach him now that I had established a connection caused me a great deal of angst.

CHAPTER 24

ALEC WAS HERE

Cindy's voice:

When Tom told me that Alec was gone, I wailed. Long, loud, anguished, and primitive wails. I could not see. My hand gripped the phone so hard I thought it would break. But I couldn't feel it. The guttural moans rushed out of my soul primitively and I hiccupped anguish through snotty sobs.

I told Tom to stay there, that he shouldn't drive when he was so upset. He could stay with friends or get a hotel.

"All I want to do is grab that cat and come home. I'll be fine driving back and I need to be with you," he said.

The tears, the sobbing, and the heartache began. Our sweet son was gone. Someone had carved up my insides. Dismembered my heart from my chest. It was unreal, not real, it could not be real. How would I ever be whole again?

We were in shock. Although this had been our biggest fear subconsciously, nothing can prepare you for the pain.

We were on the phone most of the next day, informing family and friends of what had happened. It was incredibly hard to repeat that story over and over. We texted our daughter to see if she was awake and asked if her girlfriend was with her. I then texted her girlfriend and asked her to go over to Vera's apartment to be with her for a bit, saying that it was important. Although Vera had known that Alec was in recovery, they hadn't seen each other in months. It was still a shock. I'm glad her girlfriend was there for her. Vera had a large project due that following week and she was running a photoshoot that day, which she dedicated to Alec.

Friends and family all had the same basic emotional reaction. They couldn't believe it. Many of them knew Alec had been in recovery but some didn't, and for them it was even more of a shock.

A good friend and her boyfriend came over the next day. We needed distraction and hugs from friends. We sat out on our deck, looking at the ocean and talking. Then we saw a red male tufted-head cardinal, on the side of a palm tree, just staring at us. The cardinal stayed there for twenty minutes. It was Alec, or one of our parents who'd passed, there to comfort us.

The first week was full of all the details and arrangements in planning a memorial service. All the details ran together, and we were barely coping. We got through the days by making them as busy as we could. If we stopped and thought for a second, we broke down, incapable of functioning.

One day during that first week, Tom was taking a morning walk along the road near our home. Suddenly, he saw the shadow of a bird. He looked up, and a falcon was headed straight for his head, and it circled him several times before flying off. Alec was visiting.

We were incredibly grateful to friends who came over, brought us lunch or dinner, and helped us plan the music for the service. We rented a large house to accommodate close friends and family for the weekend of the memorial service. Our dear friends stocked the house with all the meals, snacks, sweets, drinks and everything anyone could possibly want. We couldn't think, barely moved, the blur of activity streamed in front of our eyes. We talked about anything else.

The service was beautiful, and the chapel at the funeral home was full. Neither Tom nor I could speak at the service, but we wrote a homily that we asked the pastor to read. We were open and transparent about what had transpired. We made a plea that addiction needs less stigma and more research into effective treatments. And we promised ourselves that we would do something that made a difference.

After the service, Tom and I took my mother with us to the mountains. She brings me so much comfort. At ninety-three years of age, she was still busy helping others, and she wanted to be with us. My sister came a few days later. Then friends visited here and there. I am still in awe of the support we had from our friends and family. The first few months were simply a blur to me.

About a month after he died, I believe Alec came to me in my bedroom. It was morning, and I was just waking up. The sun peeping through the drawn shade was projecting light on my ceiling akin to sunrays in a picture drawn by a child. I stared at it, wondering how that particular set of light rays could come across my ceiling in precisely that way. Suddenly, I saw a soft gray shape move across the sun's rays and disappear. If I had to describe its shape, I would say it was an uneven, shadowy orb. It was gone so quickly, I, of course, wondered if I had imagined it. Then I held onto the hope that it was Alec and didn't let that go.

ALEXANDER V. GIRMAN & CYNTHIA J. GIRMAN

CHAPTER 25

SPIRITS TO CALL

Cindy's voice:

It's Alec's favorite time very early in the morning and I plea to his and my own spirit guides to channel the words through me so that they flow to the page.

"Tell me again what else you do for fun, Alec."

Alec's voice:

I like to visit the animals sometimes. I always loved animals, especially our cats and dogs. Sometimes, I visit the horses or cows too. It's awesome to visit the dinosaur souls. None of the animals have the kill instinct any longer because they don't need food. There is no reason to be afraid of any of them. I may have to visit the lions and cheetah. I know you like to see them on safari.

Sometimes I study the knowledge that I already have, especially before I go into the learning center to gain more understanding of a topic. It's like a download on my laptop from the internet, except what is stored are visions and emotions, like the way we communicate. Information is not stored in binary or numbers, or even words.

When I go exploring, I think my way there. The way I can do that is through the learning center, by gaining an understanding of the universe and beyond. Then I can think my way there. I know it's hard to understand, but if you imagine having a memory about a place you've been, it's a little like that. Only the memory is one from your knowledge or from the learning center, and you may not have experienced it directly. It may have been an experience from a past life or you may have gained knowledge of it when you came into the afterlife, or when you were learning.

I spend a lot of time learning because it's what I enjoy. When I hang out with family, we review past experiences. I've learned about the family that way. One soul can review their many past lives with all of us, then another may review theirs. I have lived many prior physical lives too, and I review those with the family.

Mom, your last medium told you that you had some very difficult times in your prior lives and that in this one, you should give yourself a break. You should experience and enjoy this life. It's true, Mom. You tend to work a lot. Make more time for yourself; get outdoors and experience. Take more walks with the puppy in nature. Go to the park. Plan more trips.

"Sometimes, Alec, if I play too much, even if it's fun activities, it stresses me out. I need my downtime, too."

It's good that you are aware of that. Build that time in too. Read more and learn. You have much to learn about the spiritual life and awakening your soul. You will be amazed at what a difference it makes to understand the true 'you'.

"I was thinking about planning a trip to see a real shaman. What do you think about that, Alec?"

I think that would be a great thing to do. Read about shaman experiences. Research specific ones and make sure they are truly what you are expecting. It could help you open your consciousness to a much broader understanding.

"Tell me again about the spirit guide and other spirits of a divine soul."

The different spirits have different roles. There is the spirit guide, the spirit that helps you make decisions or when you need help. You can plea to your own spirit guide, or you can plea to another soul's spirit guide, especially if you are asking for something that involves another soul. When you were in your last medium session, the medium suggested prayers to your sister's spirit guide to help her find path to health.

There is what we call a master spirit, who helps control all the spirits of your divine soul. There are other spirits too, like the spirit teacher guides. That's what I do. Most of the time, I teach other souls through the learning center and help more junior spirit teacher guides; sometimes I am called upon to teach a soul outside of the center. That's another level of difficulty that I'm learning more about how to do.

"I keep seeing a vision of a soul surrounding by smaller lights— are those the spirits of the divine soul?"

Yes, I am trying to help you understand. There are different spirits that each divine soul has, and they all serve a different role in the afterlife. Only some spirits can help those on the physical side. Mom, you make a plea to our spirit guides before every transcendental conversation, and they help guide us in writing.

"If I need help with a decision, and I would like some guidance toward the decision that is right for me, who would I ask for help?"

Your spirit guide of your divine soul can help you with decisions and guide you on your path. But what is the 'right decision' for you? How do you define that? Each decision could have different paths in your life. Which path do you want? The spirit guide will guide you, but can't make any decisions for you.

ALEXANDER V. GIRMAN & CYNTHIA J. GIRMAN

"How do I know what the spirit guide is guiding me toward?"

You need to open your mind and be receptive. You will then simply know. You will make the decision and feel good about it.

"But what if it's still not clear to me?"

Then it's not an easy choice. Make one and don't worry so much about it. You will be able to see what path your different choices would have led to when you do the life review in the afterlife. Sometimes human beings worry and fret too much over a single decision. Then that decision becomes way too important in their minds. In turn, it becomes difficult to make the decision because it has become so overwhelmingly important. Remember I suggested you think of life as an experience that you are having, not something that is happening to you? It's only a short experience given the eternity of the afterlife. Make the decisions that you feel are best and move on to experiencing the rest of your physical life.

You know what you need to do most of the time. You just need to do it.

"Yes, I know Alec. I just need to do it."

Physical humans are creatures of habit. Sometimes we fall into good habits or bad habits. You and Dad have your own routine every day. You both spend most of your day working. Then you spend time together but separate on your devices, Dad cooks and the two of you eat and then you watch shows on TV. Maybe think about breaking that up and doing other things. Get out of your routine.

The holidays are coming up and I know Vera is coming home for Christmas. You have told her about me, right? Does she know we are writing this book?

"Yes, she knows. Should I let her read some of it or wait until it's finished?"

I think she would be more receptive when it's finished. But if she asks to read some of it, let her read one of the chapters describing my initial experience when I passed into this realm.

You and Vera are getting along so much better now. I'm glad she's more in touch. I think she will be happier when she meets more people where she is. She likes her job. I want her to be happy. I wish I was nicer to her when I was on the physical side.

"I know, son. You were being a teenage brother."

Still, I could have been nicer. We were close when we were little but grew apart as we got older. I suppose that's not uncommon, but I didn't live long enough to have the chance to become close again, like many siblings do. I will see her again someday. I will greet her when she comes home.

"Can you suggest what I should do about my brother, Alec? It seems like he wants to be mad at us, or at least at me."

Be kind to him. He is not well. Try to see things from his side. He expects a lot to be given to him, but that's how he's wired. It's not a choice he made consciously to be that way. Try to be kind even when he's angry.

"That's good advice for anyone."

Yes, it's all about love and forgiveness and acceptance. The sooner you accept that this is the way he is, the more you will forgive and forget.

"Thank you for that, Alec."

Your spirit guide can help guide you in your interactions with him, or with other physical humans that you struggle with. Not all mortals are kind, and few humans are actually aware and open to the broader understanding of physical and non-physical life.

"Are there other spirits and souls around me, like you are?"

Don't be afraid, Mom. There are no malevolent spirits around you. There are other spirits that love you that surround you, though. Like your father, grandparents, uncles and aunts, and friends. Meditate. Open your mind and let them in. It will improve your well-being and give you support and confidence in your life. Try a course on meditation, maybe. It might help. Even an online one that guides you through it could help.

It's almost time for me to go. The sun is starting to rise, and I have things to do. Until we write again.

CHAPTER 26

QUIET YOUR MIND TO AWAKEN

Cindy's voice:

I plea to the spirit guides and teaching spirits of Alec and my own divine self, to please help me in writing the truth, in putting the words on the page that communicate what should be shared.

"Alec, you used to enjoy flying, with Flight Simulators, if nothing else. Can you fly over the planets, or is it all only teleporting?"

Alec's voice:

Travel is all by what you might call "teleporting". Although it's not exactly what physical humans might think of. If I want to teleport slowly from one place to another place, it takes a great deal of concentration so that I don't go too fast. I would almost need to teleport in steps, then I get the sensation of flying. And we aren't hovering over something. That's a human concept. We are there in it.

"Ah, I see. Can you hover if you want to?"

Yes, I can, I must teleport to be on that plane. It's all about dimensions.

"How do you enjoy the beauty of the afterlife if you can't see the broad view? Sometimes when you are in a new place, you can't see the beauty of the broader picture."

I know what you mean, but again, it's a human concept of only being in one 'place'. We are everywhere. We see and feel it all.

"How do you know where to teleport if you haven't been everywhere in the afterlife?"

You just know. Remember that we get that big download at the beginning of the afterlife, and then we learn. As we learn, we understand more and more about the dimensions and how to use them. There isn't a 'place' in the spiritual realm. There are different planes or dimensions that we teleport to.

"What about the angels? Do they really have wings? That's probably a silly question."

Angels earn their status. Remember I told you that angel wings were a human concept that has been passed down for ages? They don't have wings, but they can teleport through time and space on the physical side. They earn their robes, which are more elaborate the closer the angel is to higher beings, and to Jesus and God. One day I hope to earn an angel's robe.

"What was that noise, Alec?"

Chico is knocking things over. He wants a treat, Mom.

"It's the middle of the night!"

Cats are nocturnal, Mom, remember?

The night is slowly fading and soon the sun will rise. When it does, take in the beauty of the sunrise over the ocean. It is one of God's most beautiful creations, the sun rising and setting, and the moon as well. Get out of your desk chair and go outside if you need to, to view the beauty.

"I am seeing my aunts in my mind today."

Yes, they want to be with you. They want you to pay attention to what is being communicated. They want you to stop working so much and experience life. Don't waste it working. Get outdoors, walk, and hike. Enjoy nature. Life is made of experiences. Every experience you have leaves some sort of imprint on you. Go and have the kind of experiences that you hold on to and treasure. Remember what Sylvia communicated during the medium session? Don't carry that grief and worry and fear around with you. Let all that go and enjoy your experience in this physical life.

"That sounds like good advice, and you've been telling me that all along. It's time to take the first step. I will do that this weekend. I will start practicing meditation with my singing bowl."

Physical beings always look up when they are thinking of their loved ones' departed spirits. We aren't up, we are all around you. But if it helps to look up, that's fine.

"It's hard to think about a spirit or soul being all around me. It's easier to think of a soul in one spot. I guess it's the limitation of my physical human brain. How can I expand that?"

Awakening of your soul. Enlightenment. Research those retreats. You would find it amazing. It would change your life, your entire focus. It would give you a new direction. Be careful though. There are those on the physical side that will claim to be able to guide you in enlightenment, but they have greed and only want your money. Choose wisely who you work with. And read about it ahead of time so you know what to expect.

"What about shows or YouTube videos? Is that worth doing?"

It's up to you. It would teach you more about it, but you may not reach the state that a live retreat might offer.

"How will I know a good one from a bad one? There must be some that are authentic, and others that are fake?"

Yes, be careful how you choose them. Read the reviews. And ask for guidance from your guiding and teaching spirits.

Awakening your soul would help you understand much of what I have been trying to communicate. The retreats on awakening your soul would first teach you how to quiet your mind and meditation techniques. They would go deeper and deeper into this state, and then you would invoke the spirit guides of your soul to guide you and help you with the understanding of All Things being connected and the planes of existence. You would love it. It would help you find your future.

"My future is going to be very different from what I have imagined, isn't it, Alec?"

Yes, but it depends on what you choose. You will have the future that you choose. But remember that I am always there with you. And call on your spirit guides to help you. That's why they are there.

"Alec, it feels like you are winding down. Is that for today, or are you winding down for these transcendental conversations? I don't want to give up these sessions with you, Alec. I have enjoyed the connection so much."

I have enjoyed these sessions too, but I have things to do on different planes. I will be with you, though. All you have to do is call.

Cindy's voice:

In my mind, I see a beautiful pastel view of the sun in a pink sky, over hills with a river running through it, similar to images from before. Alec sends me beautiful images and I wish I could paint them so I could remember them forever.

CHAPTER 27

WISHING I WAS THERE

Cindy's voice:

Two and a half months after Alec's passing, we went to Chapel Hill, North Carolina, to our friends' long-standing annual gathering for New Year's Eve. We weren't really feeling up to a party, but our friends convinced us it would be good to be around people who care. As we arrived early, we went to Alec's favorite restaurant for his favorite meal: cheeseburgers and fries. Tom went inside to order, and I snagged the only table left outside. We were still observing masks indoors because of COVID-19, and luckily, the weather was warm despite the time of year.

As I sat down at the table and put my purse down, I spotted a penny right in front of me. I knew it was a sign from heaven, like the dimes, feathers or cardinals we occasionally spotted. Tears ran down my face unabated as I picked it up and kissed it. Alec was there with us at his favorite restaurant.

We were in a fog of grief for several months before Tom went to Panama for a birding trip and met Maria, who insisted on paying for our first session with a medium. I had been obsessively worrying about whether Alec was ok. As a mother who had constantly worried about him because of his ADHD and Asperger's, and then his addiction, I wanted to know how he was doing in the afterlife. The first medium assuaged my concerns and convinced me he was in bliss.

While Tom was in Panama, two friends of mine came to help me take care of our dog, Lexi, who had just had surgery to remove rectal cancer. I couldn't leave Lexi right after her surgery while she was still recovering.

While they were there, I opened the bag of treats to give one to Lexi, and out fell a dime. I was elated and fell to my knees crying out, "It's Alec!"

We saw signs at other times too. Dimes and pennies that we would find. Smells of Alec's natural essence in the kitchen on a random day. Cardinals that we would see or hear from our deck. Each time we grasped for hope that it was Alec, there with us, all around us, giving us a sign.

Seven months after Alec passed, I was standing in the kitchen by the dining table, sad and thinking of Alec and my father.

I looked at Tom and said through tears, "I just want to go be with Dad and Alec."

Tom gave me a big hug, and I sobbed.

"I feel that way too sometimes," he admitted. Just to be with Alec one more time.

About four months later, after a mediumship session, when my grandmother came forward to reassure me, I had a visitation during the night. I had woken to an intense feeling that someone was just outside our bedroom in the hallway and coming toward us. I grabbed the covers and held them tight with eyes open wide, terrified. I sat up, wanting to wake up Tom but knowing I didn't have time. Then they were in the room but the door hadn't moved.

Suddenly, I was certain that my maternal grandmother and grandfather were beside the bed. I then experienced what at the time I attributed to fear, but later would know was a spirit passing through me. Both my grandmother and grandfather went through me over the span of a few seconds, then were gone. I felt nauseous and tense, disoriented and light-headed. I had such a strong reaction that I woke up Tom, who was sleeping beside me. It was difficult getting back to sleep. At the time, I didn't know that this was how it felt to have a spirit pass through you, much less two. Now I know how it feels to have two spirits pass through me as well as one, which Alec showed me during one of our conversations.

Not much later, I started researching transcranial magnetic stimulation (TEMS) and transcranial direct current stimulation (TDCS) of the brain. One of Alec's inpatient residential counselors in Raleigh had sent us a link to a video that was discussing some research on the use of it to normalize brain waves and reduce craving. Evidently, brain waves are modified even after early misuse of opioids. I wanted to understand what studies had been done, perhaps because of my scientific biostatistical and epidemiological background in clinical trials and drug development. I wanted to see if there was a pattern in the frequency, intensity and other parameters that would point to how it should be implemented in addiction. Unfortunately, there was no pattern, only a lot of variability in results of small studies. I spoke with neurologist colleagues and friends, two of which said that they would help in any way they could. Then I spoke with two substance use disorders (SUDs) epidemiologists about where the field was and whether they would be interested in participating in a grant application for government funding for a large randomized clinical trial in this area. However, it wasn't until fall, just after the first anniversary of Alec's death, that I finally got some traction.

Based on a newsletter from the translational medicine research group at UNC, I learned they had formed a new brain center at UNC, with some of the top neurologists in the nation, to focus on Alzheimer's disease and dementia. I emailed one of the translational medicine group co-directors that I knew well and asked if he knew of anyone doing work in transcranial magnetic or electrical current stimulation for substance use disorders, and he immediately put me in touch with an enthusiastic researcher who was using this approach for depression. In a matter of fifteen minutes, I had received the newsletter, asked about researchers in the area, emailed the researcher, and the researcher had responded with times he was available so I could set up a call with him. I was excited that I had found what seemed like the perfect researcher in this field. It felt like I was on the right path.

I got up from my laptop, took a deep breath of air, and when I looked down, there was a dime on the end of my desk. What a great fifteen minutes! And Alec was there with me, too. I then went into the closet near my office a few minutes later, and there was another dime! Alec was indeed with me, and excited about this meeting to discuss research into effective treatments for substance use disorders.

CHAPTER 28

FIND PURPOSE THROUGH HEART AND MIND

Cindy's voice:

S ending a plea up to the spirit guides and spirit teacher guides of both Alec and my own divine soul, I sit at the keys, hoping that the words flow to the page.

"Alec, you know I have had chronic lower back pain for thirty years, and now, Achilles tendinopathy and knee issues. It is especially painful after long rides in the car. Are there spirits of my divine soul that I can ask for relief and healing physically, not only emotionally?"

Alec's voice:

You can ask your Master spirit to help you and your healing spirit guide, to guide you to health. If it's not something that you are to learn and experience, they may be able to help. I know you experienced chronic pain my whole physical life and that can't be fun. Try to seek some ancient healers. They may be able to help. Unfortunately, modern medicine can't really help your specific lumbar issue because the vertebrae is sitting right on your nerve and there is no disc left.

"What would you like to share in the book that you haven't already?"

I want to make sure that a few things are clear. In the afterlife, we feel emotion and have knowledge and understanding. We have consciousness, but it's not the same as on the physical side. We don't get physical signs and symptoms from the emotions. If we are sad, which is rare, we don't have the heaviness in the heart and the lethargy that accompanies that physically. It's the emotion itself in our consciousness, so it's different.

Also, negative emotions are transient. They don't last long because of the unconditional love and acceptance here. It's difficult to carry negative feelings for long, but we do have them when we have certain memories.

"What is it like to remember your past lives, Alec? How is that done? It seems like it would be overwhelming. And how many past lives are you remembering?"

It's not like the memories of all the past lives descend on you at once. They are there and you can seek them out. It's like a stack in computer code. You can access information anywhere in the stack at any time. Some of us have thousands of past lives, going back to the beginning of time for some of us. Mine do not go back nearly that far, but I have past lives from thousands of years ago. Some of my past lives were not physical humans, but animals. Some of yours may have been animals too. They don't typically live as long as humans.

"Can you not see the past lives of my soul?"

If I try, I'm sure I could. There is so much that I am learning in other areas that I haven't tried to understand your past lives. I am still trying to wrap my consciousness around my own.

"What sort of experiences did you have in past lives, Alec? Can you share that?"

The past lives vary dramatically. It all depends on what my divine soul needed to experience.

"Would I understand the connectedness of All Things if I studied quantum physics? You know how I always struggled to understand physics!"

Yes, it would help. Although even quantum physics isn't going to give you everything, it will help you understand it better. The more you can learn while on the physical side, the easier it will be when you arrive here. But don't spend all your time on it. You are there for a reason and you need to have the experiences that you were sent to have.

"How do I know what those experiences are?"

Open your mind. Meditate. Be mindful and listen to your heart and mind. You can ask for guidance from your spirits. They will give you signs if you ask them. They cannot change the course of your physical life, but they can give you guidance. Go to one of those awakening retreats that we talked about before. It will help you find your purpose. Your last medium can help too, or perhaps the shaman since you mentioned visiting one.

"Should Dad go as well?"

Not to the same one. You need to be there for yourself and without distraction. But he should go separately to one so that he understands his own purpose.

"What if my purpose doesn't involve Dad?"

Then you would have a choice. You are projecting your fears, Mom. Don't do that. Let those go. It would be good to let them go before you attend one of those retreats.

"How could I increase my frequency?"

You may be able to do that by awakening your soul. I can't tell you how. But it is possible for some physical humans to achieve a higher frequency. Not quite as high as in the afterlife. It's how out-of-body experiences occur. You tried to have out-of-body experiences and time travel when you were a teenager, a long time ago. Think back to that. Did you ever achieve it?

"I tried, and a few times, it felt like I did, but I was never sure it wasn't just memories of where I'd been before."

You were trying to travel to a place then, not really a different time. Some physical humans have tried to travel in time to a future or past state. Others attempt to travel through space. Try traveling through your consciousness to understand how you are connected to everything.

"Can my spirit guides help me with that?"

Yes, they can. Wait until after you have let go of your fears and attended the awakening retreat. You will have much better results.

"Can I ask my spirits to help me understand what I should do next year? Where should I travel? What should I do about work? Who should I meet with?"

Yes, but you will understand that through your awakening retreat and finding your purpose as well.

Today, you should go outdoors. Walk the puppy.

"I will, Alec. He is such a good puppy for us. When I think of travel through space, I think of flying. I have the sensation of soaring over the earth and up into the stars, and then I don't know where to go."

You will know that soon enough. You don't have to rush things. Enjoy the journey, Mom. First, you need to let go of your fears. Make a list of things you are afraid of. Don't overthink it. Make a list rapidly of whatever comes to mind. You can add to it as you think of things later if you do it on your smartphone. You should have well over twenty or so fears.

"That's a lot. What other advice do you have for me, Alec?"

Pace yourself. You tend to dive into the deep end of the pool when you take on something new. Not this time. Wade in from the shallow end and absorb it all slowly. You will have a much deeper experience emotionally that way.

"That's good advice. You know me well. When I think of the connectedness of All Things, I start to get overwhelmed. Is it overwhelming to be connected to everything, other souls and animals and trees and mountains and all?"

It's not overwhelming because it is an understanding of All Things. I am connected with living things as well as things you might consider non-living but that grow slowly. Being connected to them allows me to understand how they evolve. Understanding is connectedness, and being connected means you understand.

"What about other souls? When you are connected to all your ancestors, are you able to see their immediate past life and all their other lives too? If you are connected to an infinite number of ancestors, doesn't that get to be too much?"

Our consciousness is expanded beyond your physical capability. We can handle infinite dimensions and infinite experiences at the same time. You are thinking with the limitations of the physical brain.

"It's hard for us humans to imagine."

It will all become clear in time.

"How is Papa? It's almost Christmas and I really miss you and my dad, your Papa."

I will always be there, Mom. I am with you, all around you. You need not worry about that. It's a fear you can let go. You have so many fears and that drives your anxiety. Acknowledge them and let them go. Have a ceremony on the beach or in the mountains where you throw them away.

"I am hearing a tone that is calming and seeing my singing bowl in my mind."

Yes, both will help you throw away those fears. Mediation can really help. Starting each morning with gratitude and positivity will help, too.

"A lot of focus on me today. What about your father? Vera? And Nana and my sister? Friends?"

It would be great for Dad to see the medium that you saw. It would help him, I think. You've been worried about him. He will be alright, but he needs to go through some grieving by himself. You have come much further through the mediums and by writing this book. He will get there, but it will take time.

Vera is focused on Vera right now, like anyone twenty-two years old. She had a lot of anxiety, but she is much better now. Be patient with her. She is coming to realizations about herself.

Nana is bored most of the time. She enjoys reading and movies with you and your sister, but otherwise, she has little to do. She does reach out to much of the family that is still living. It's great that she keeps in touch with them. She spends the rest of her time reading, but that's good because it keeps her mind sharp.

Aunt Kathy is overwhelmed. Talk to her about letting go of some things. Plea to her guiding and teaching spirits every day to help her find her path toward a healthy and fulfilling life. She loves that granddaughter!

Your college friends are all fine. I sort of grew up with them. They mean a lot to me. I am with them too.

"Describe to me the beauty of the afterlife and heaven again, Alec. Is it all beautiful? Are there parts of the afterlife that are not so beautiful?"

It's so beautiful, Mom. Whatever your idea of beauty is, it is here, and so much more. The colors are magnificent. In the learning center, we can view the beauty and understand how God created it all. Everything is God and God is everything. God is Love.

When you envision beautiful scenes like what would be on a Christmas card or postcard, you might find something similar here.

"Does every soul see the same beautiful scenes?"

It depends on their enlightenment and understanding. Not everyone takes the learning to understand the afterlife, heaven and its beauty. It takes millennia to understand it all. But all of us understand that the beauty here is unparalleled.

"Are there views that are mundane, or is everything absolute beauty?"

Everything that God created is beauty.

It's time for you to go back to sleep. Yesterday you realized you had seen your dreams before, that they were perhaps memories. You don't often remember your dreams, but sometimes reading something will prompt a memory. Hold on to those. Your dreams are a gateway to understanding, even if negative.

Cindy's voice:

Alec said my dreams are a gateway to understanding. I rarely remember my dreams. I used to keep a journal by my bed so I could write dreams down to help me remember them. That helped a lot.

But the dream that I remembered that Alec mentioned was a nightmare in which I was being chased by someone I didn't know that terrified me. That doesn't bode well for letting go of my fears.

I wonder if reawakening my soul would help me retrieve and remember my dreams. I wonder if I could selectively remember the ones that weren't nightmares! Something to think about.

CHAPTER 29

HUMAN AMNESIA AND AURA COLORS

Cindy's voice:

The holidays came and all the bustle of getting ready for Christmas resurfaced all our memories of Alec. His stocking hangs empty by the fireplace. We have a small special tree we call the "Alec tree," and we decorate it with special ornaments that have his name on them or that he made in pre-school and kindergarten. Friends give us ornaments to hang on the tree that remind them of Alec, like a cheeseburger ornament, and a rainbow. We cherish those and I like to think that he does too.

It's been days since I had a transcendental conversation with Alec, and I am hoping he can join me. I plea to the guiding and teaching spirits of my divine self, to help the words flow from the spiritual realm to my fingers.

Alec's voice:

I was there with all of you on Christmas Eve and Christmas Day. I know you enjoyed the love of family. It is so important.

"Alec, are there special occasions in the afterlife? Do you celebrate some of the same holidays that we do? Are birthdays acknowledged, like the day Jesus was born in his physical life?"

No, we don't have birthday celebrations of physical lives. Our physical lives are so short compared to the infinity of souls, angels and higher beings. There is no time in the afterlife, so we don't have days. We do celebrate God and His creation, but that's done on a regular basis by all of us.

"When I get flashes of déjà vu or like I've been in the exact same situation and heard and seen the exact same thing before, is that something to do with the spiritual realm? Is it a memory from a prior physical life or spiritual life, or from the future, or is it from a dream?"

It could be any of those. Most likely, it is from a past life or from a future that you dreamed about. Mortals dream frequently, but only remember them rarely. However, your consciousness remembers them and when you are in the same situation, it triggers a feeling of being there before.

"How do we exist as souls? Is it possible that souls can be tangible? I know you said it was very difficult to be on a single physical plane so that mortals can see a soul, but if they give off energy, shouldn't they be detectable somehow??"

Souls are detectable as energy, with the right technology. Even though you don't see them, there is energy, and if you have the right tool, you can detect the energy. That's why people can detect how many 'ghosts' are in a haunted house. Those are spirits with remaining issues they need to resolve, and they are not yet at peace.

Mom, you seem anxious today. You're worried I'm going to not be accessible, but I'm here right now. Be present. I will always be with you. I am around you and in everything. All you need to do is call me. I will be right there. Calm down, ok?

"It's great advice, Alec. I love that you are there and I can talk to you. I have another question. People have described waves of information in the afterlife. Is that what it's like, Alec? Does everything move in waves? Is that how information is transmitted, in waves?"

A lot of the afterlife involves waves of information. The 'download' that I received happened right after I passed over to this side? It came in waves, but quick waves. Sometimes the communication between souls comes in waves, especially if it's a lot of information. The entire infrastructure of communication and information is based on waves of energy. And we, as souls, are energy. Imagine the digital 'waves' of sound that you see on a stereo system. You can think of communication of information as those waves. We exist in many waves, almost like being in the ocean with the rhythmic movement and sound of the waves.

"Have you ever been around us and traveled through us, Alec? Can you do that? I've read that people may not sense it as a spirit passing through them at the time, but they may gasp?"

Yes, I have gone through you when I was trying to get your attention, and yes, you stop and sense something, and usually gasp. You haven't been aware that it was me before, but now that you know, maybe you'll recognize it.

"If there are so many souls, how do they keep from bumping into each other?"

That's funny, Mom. I'm imagining souls bopping into each other like a pinball machine! No, we don't bump into each other because each soul has their own energy field and aura that surrounds them and keeps them from bumping into other balls of energy.

"Alec, did you just go right through me? I was dizzy and lightheaded, like something was off."

Yes, that was me. Now you know what it feels like.

"Wow, I really should recognize that now! It was obvious and strong. I can't believe I didn't recognize it before!

Alec, do different souls have different colors as part of their aura? What do the different colors reflect?"

It's complicated, but the simple answer is that the colors reflect different roles and levels of learning and growth. For example, in a spirit teacher guide role, we have different colors that reflect whether we are newly a teacher guide, intermediate, senior or a master level teacher guide.

"And what color are you, Alec?"

My aura color is blueish since I'm an intermediate spirit teacher guide. As you get into the angels, there are different colors to reflect the different levels up through the archangels. The stronger colors are closer to the One, the Higher Being we call God, whose light is so intense, only the highest beings can be in His presence.

Spirits have a different color depending on the job they do. Most souls are white. But as an example for teacher guides, a junior teacher is yellow moving into golden, intermediate is blue, starting out light blue and moving across the spectrum of blue as we advance to a dark blue, almost purple. This corresponds to different wave frequencies. The higher the spirit dwells, the quicker the waves become. The higher beings have the most intense rich colors.

"Are you an 'old' soul, Alec? How many lives have you had?"

I had many prior lives before, too many to count. That's why I am an intermediate teacher. I was a teacher guide long before I was in my physical life as your son. I suppose you would call me an 'old soul' but I am not nearly as old as the 'elders' that go so far back in time in their past lives. It's hard to fathom.

"Do souls laugh and have a sense of humor? I bet you get along well if they do. You've always had such a great sense of humor, Alec."

Of course. We all laugh and kid around. It is part of the sense of bliss here to laugh and be happy. Otherwise, being serious and somber all the time would be suffocating. We especially do that in our primary soul groups and with our relatives and family.

"How do souls pass through into the physical world? Are there openings? Like black holes or something?"

There are thresholds that are part of the creation of the physical and spiritual world. What God created is amazing - the worlds are such that there can be passing between them to enhance the learning and growth opportunities. But very few physical humans can do this or know it exists. Mostly for humans in physical life on earth, it is a one-way ticket.

"How do you find the spirits of souls that you want to hang out with, Alec? Like family. Have you found friends?"

It's not something that you have to work hard to do. Family is there when you arrive here in the afterlife, and you connect with them immediately. At least a soul's family and ancestors. My birth family and all your relatives and Dad's too were right there. I was young when I died, so I didn't know any friends that died while I was on earth.

"Have you made friends while there? Are there friends from your prior lives?"

I have connected with so many through my teaching, Mom, especially all the spirits that I met when I taught as a junior teacher guide. After my formal evaluation of my learnings from this past physical life, I was reappointed to my role as an intermediate spirit teacher guide. That means reconnection with other teacher guides at the intermediate level and receiving my assigned soul groups to oversee junior teacher guide instruction. I am also connected with soul groups of my friends from prior lives and family, of course. Soul or spirit groups are formed by where they are in learning and how they think, so that there is some commonality among the members of the group. They are drawn to each other almost like waves based on the intensity of the spirit light. There are many soul groups that you connect with.

I no longer have awkwardness socially, so I have made plenty of friends. It is nice. We have ancestors and many loved ones from our last physical life, but also prior lives. We also have soul groups of people who were friends in our prior lives, not only the ones I have with ancestors.

"That's cool. So you reconnect as souls with friends from prior lives, and you have shared experiences from when you were both on the physical side?"

Yes, that's right. And we all can remember and laugh about things. It's nice to reminisce about our prior lives, but also share what we've discovered about the afterlife. Our soul groups have members that often have similar thinking and level of learning. We usually agree in our thinking, which is why we are connected in the first place. But occasionally, there are disagreements in our discussions and learning. There are ways to resolve those calmly and lovingly if initial communication does not.

"How large is your soul group? Is your soul group made up of only teacher guides, or of friends and family from prior lives, or what?"

I hang out with other teacher guides as a soul group, and it's relatively small because I'm at the intermediate level. As you move up in level, the soul group gets smaller and smaller. I told you I am part of many soul groups. I have the family and ancestor soul groups, multiple ones because of the different sides of your family and Dad's. Also, the soul groups of my birthmother and birthfather. Then I have soul groups of friends from prior lives that I've been with through many, many incarnations. We know each other well and are close. We hang out with our primary soul group most of the time when we are not teaching or learning, but we are connected to many other soul groups and relatives and can communicate with them.

"Is there anything else that you specifically would like to tell the physical world, Alec?"

It is all about love. Love is all. The physical human life is merely a small experience and there is a reason for that physical life. They need to experience something in that physical life. They are there to learn, and part of the learning is supposed to be for them to understand that love is everything. If you have love, you can get beyond anything.

Tell them to enjoy their life. Stop chasing monetary gains and power and do things that you enjoy. So many people are in jobs that they can't stand, so they can buy a big house and a fancy car, or so they can accomplish some big achievement. That's not what they are supposed to be learning with their experience in the physical world. They should focus on their passions, activities that they enjoy and what makes them feel glad to be alive. For most people, that isn't building their bank account, but for some reason, mortals think that's what they are supposed to be doing.

They should focus on creating joy, communing with nature, getting together with those they love. Human beings in their physical lives should seek a greater understanding of themselves, who they are, what makes them excited, and how they can give back to the world. If they don't know their purpose, they should seek it out.

Like I've said before, understanding your true self is the most important endeavor you can undertake, and all mortals should undertake it, but they usually don't. Many people die without even trying to understand who they are and what they want. It is sad that so many die before understanding their purpose. Those are the souls that usually want to go back on earth to have another experience where they might learn what they need to learn to evolve their divine soul.

"Why do humans in a physical life have amnesia about learnings and memories from their prior lives, especially their last one? Why shouldn't they know what they are supposed to be learning?"

It is God's design so that physical humans feel in control of their lives and can make choices. If they all knew what the purpose of their experience was and what they needed to learn, they would do so quickly and not live a long life that perhaps was their destiny. Amnesia ensures that they learn on their own. I hope someday that mankind on the physical side learns that greed, wealth, and power are not what they were incarnated for. Life is an experience to be enjoyed and to learn from, not a competition.

I think you should wrap up the book now. You have enough material, and the messages are there. I have tried to communicate as much as I could about my journey since I passed to this realm. The blissful and intense love and acceptance that we all feel here engulfs us and is the most wonderful, beatific feeling. So much stronger than a feeling or emotion because of its intensity. I wish I could describe it better. The infinite dimensions and connectedness of everything are also difficult to describe because you are bound by earthly dimensions. We communicate with other souls through thought and emotion in so many dimensions!

I've tried to describe the beauty here, but it is so much more than my words can convey. There are so many magnificent views and all it takes is to think of it, and we are there in it. It is so amazing.

Love is all. To have the kind of love we have in the afterlife means that you have unconditional acceptance and forgiveness of all others. That is rare for mortals to achieve.

God created earth for physical manifestations of humans to enjoy and live healthy, rewarding lives and to learn and grow from their experience on the physical side. Those learnings are the ones your divine soul believed were needed for continued growth in the spiritual realm. It is sad that mortals don't understand that. I hope you will understand after your retreat. During your retreat, you will be asked to try to define your purpose in life. That purpose, once you learn it, will guide you in your choices for the rest of your physical life.

"It feels like this is goodbye in a way, and it is making me sad."

It is not goodbye. You can still talk with me. I am always with you and always will be. If you call me, I will be there. But I have a role to fulfill in teaching, and you need to finish the book and get it in print. I will be excited to see that. The book is a nice reflection of my experience without being too morbid, and a nice depiction of how I have seen the afterlife.

I only wish we could connect and communicate on a higher level so that you could understand more. But the physical life on earth is on a lower frequency dimension. Maybe someday we can meet on the same frequency, and I will see you in the afterlife when it's your time.

Look out the window, Mom. See the colors of the sunrise over the mountains? It is beautiful, sort of like what I see in the afterlife in some dimensions, with those soft clouds over the orange-red streaks. Perhaps that's why I see some of the views that I see, because I really liked the mountains when you moved there.

Cindy's voice:

And in my mind, I saw gently rolling hills, almost cloudlike, with warm browns and greens and lavenders strung through them, and beautiful clouds on top of which sat a night sky of deep blue with so many stars and planets, it was almost bright even without a moon in sight. And then I saw what looked like an orb of light. No wings, only an oblong orb form of light, with fuzzy edges. For a second or two. And then it was gone.

I took my fingers off the keys and said to myself, "I love you, Alec. Maybe someday we can write together again. I'd like that."

EPILOGUE

S everal weeks after the first anniversary of our son's death, I started writing this book. The writing took place for thirty to ninety minutes in the early morning, when the veil between the physical and spiritual world is supposedly thinnest, on mostly consecutive days until after the first draft was done almost exactly two months later.

Some may wonder how I gained an independent connection with Alec after the three successful medium sessions (see Details of Medium Sessions). It was automatic writing, although I didn't think of it that way in the beginning. I sat down with a pen, expecting, and hoping for something, anything, from him. And he delivered. I got down as much as possible on pages for later editing. However, after completing the book, I was compelled to keep most of the words that came to me, so I left the communications from Alec raw and original, except to combine some passages that would have been redundant and editing for flow.

I should note that the timing was right for me to connect with Alec. My mind was more open after the medium sessions, which helped me heal a bit from the intense grief. Profound grief inhibits connection with the spiritual realm, and I needed a calm, open mind without deep sadness clouding it. Had I tried before the medium sessions and understanding how happy he was in the afterlife; I don't think we would have connected.

Someone told me that the descriptions in this book are like what they witnessed in a near death experience. This makes me feel less alone and strengthens my belief in what Alec was communicating. Some of the information portrayed here may not be consistent with what you as a reader have been taught or what you believe. As a Christian raised Methodist, I realize people have different beliefs and ideas of what heaven is like. This is merely one depiction from the perspective of someone dear to me who passed and communicated it to me. It is not intended to change anyone's beliefs, but rather to give the perspective of the first author, my son, communicating from the afterlife. Hopefully, it will also encourage readers to think and wonder.

Through my transcendental conversations with Alec, I have come to believe that part of our purpose on earth as physical humans is to learn to overcome our fears and to love all beings with full acceptance of what and who those beings are. As has been stated by author Reginald Gray,

We are not human beings having a spiritual experience–we are spiritual beings having a human experience.–Reginald Gray, Messages from Beyond the Veil: Spiritual Guidance for our Human Experience, Gilbert, AZ: Astralis Media Group, 2017.

I believe the messages from Alec are clear. We are in physical human flesh to experience our lives to the fullest and to learn that love conquers everything. This involves overcoming our fears and changing our measures of success and wealth that are least important to those that focus on love, forgiveness, and acceptance of all beings. It is not the duration of one's life that is important but the measure of charity, helping and giving in love. I also think a strong message was to live this gift of life to your fullest. If we live today in love and light, tomorrow will bring more of that. Sorrow makes that difficult, but joy brings joy. I must learn to find joy in my life every day.

Since my transcendental conversations with Alec, I have found a great deal more peace. My heart still aches for my son, and I will grieve him for the rest of my life, but there is substantial comfort in knowing that he is at peace and in a state of pure bliss, unconditional love, and acceptance. Grief is a lifelong endeavor when we lose people we love deeply, but I know I will be with them again. I also know that Alec is with me, all around me, and that I can call on him as well as my guardian angel and spirit guides when I need to. After the conversations with Alec, I have been doing exactly that, more and more. My life and my outlook have changed. I am a different person than I was before my transcendental conversations with Alec because I see things differently, in a completely different light than I did before. This spiritual wellness is especially noticeable during meditation and when I talk with Alec in my mind.

I have an appointment with a world-renowned shaman in mere weeks from my writing of these words, and I hope to continue my spiritual growth and journey until it is my time. This all gives me hope, and I no longer yearn to be with Alec and my father too soon. Readers will be happy to know that I indeed found my air pods as soon as I sent the manuscript to my early readers for feedback.

I do not claim that every word written in this book is true, nor that every word has come from the spiritual realm. I can, however, say that the words in these chapters came to me after I put in a prayer to the spirit guides of my own divine self and my son's divine soul, asking them to funnel through me these words that should be shared. Further, aside from the light in the tunnel and the greeting by relatives and friends, much of what Alec communicated was unfamiliar to me. This is my own healing journey and a description of Alec's journey to the Afterlife. I believe everyone experiences something different when they pass from the physical to the spiritual world, consistent with what would be a beautiful experience for them. I have not studied the metaphysical world, and minimally encountered people who have, other than the three medium sessions described next. At the encouragement of the second medium, I read a book about the afterlife that greatly intrigued me (The Afterlife of Billy Fingers: How My Bad-Boy Brother Proved to Me There's Life After Death, Annie Kagan, Hampton Roads Publishing, 2013). I ordered more books to read but didn't read them until after this book was mostly complete.

I was eager to publish what was communicated to me by Alec on those many wonderful mornings during our transcendental conversations. I hope to continue to communicate with Alec, and I am happy to know that he is thriving in the afterlife. It may take automatic writing in the wee hours of the day to achieve that. I am thrilled that we made this connection, and I hope I have done him justice in these pages.

One early reader thought this book could affect those with severe clinical depression who may be contemplating taking their own life. This book is intended to give hope to those who fear death or have lost loved ones. We have much to learn and experience, and to love, and we need to live out our life's purpose.

For those who are dealing with depression that is leading to thoughts of suicide, call 988, or call 1 800 273-TALK (8255), or the National Hopeline Network at 1-800-SUICIDE (784-2433). You can **also text HOME to 741741** to connect with a volunteer Crisis Counselor. For those in crisis due to substance abuse and in need of mental health services, call 1-800-662-HELP (4357), or you can call the National **Alliance on Mental Illness (NAMI):** 1-800-950-NAMI (6264).

The opioid crisis began long before the COVID-19 pandemic, and restriction of prescription opioids turned users to synthetic opiates and street drugs. The isolation, loneliness and increase in mental illness during the pandemic drove the crisis to terrifying heights. By profession, I am a scientist with training in biostatistics and epidemiology, and I have spent over forty years working in drug development, to design observational studies and clinical trials to help bring new medicines to people more efficiently. Our experience with Alec during his twenty months in recovery taught Tom and me that new approaches to treating substance use disorders are sorely needed. While cognitive-behavioral therapy is the gold standard for the treatment of substance use disorders and alcoholism, it does not treat the physical aspects of the disease. The cravings are still there, despite the counseling and group therapy. For example, the brain waves in substance use disorders are purportedly modified, particularly during decision-making to use, which creates continued cravings. Researchers and professors at the University of North Carolina are testing transcranial alternating current brain stimulation to shift those brain waves and possibly reduce the craving associated with SUD and alcoholism. Such technology has been successful with other mental illnesses, such as depression, and has promise in addiction and possibly autism. With a reduction in cravings, cognitive-behavioral therapy and group therapy have a chance to be so much more effective.

My husband and I are collaborating with researchers on this technology, hoping to identify algorithms or approaches to individualize the appropriate parameters related to the dose of such technology based on their brain waves during tasks simulating drug use decision-making. With this identified, the hope is to apply for funding to support a large randomized clinical trial to demonstrate effectiveness. We hope that this technology can be an affordable way to treat those living with substance use disorders and allow them to live normal lives.

Alec died due to toxicity from mitragynine and 7-hydroxymitragynine, the two major alkaloids of kratom. We think it was kratom combined with another substance, but toxicity from these two alkaloids was deemed to have caused his death. Kratom is a dangerous opioid that is on the market with no regulation by the United States Food and Drug Administration. There has been a rash of overdose and deaths associated with its use in the past five years. It should be taken off the market, and at least regulated by the Food & Drug Administration as a controlled substance. In most states, kratom is legal with no restrictions on age for buyers. This means anyone, including teens, can enter a vape or smoke shop and purchase it. Other states have a restriction to age over twenty-one years. A few states have banned its use or made it illegal, but too few have done that. Many people are under the mistaken impression that it is safe, simply because it is on the market with no restrictions. That couldn't be further from the truth.

To learn more, see

https://www.fda.gov/news-events/public-health-focus/fda-and-kratom.

DETAILS OF
THE MEDIUM SESSIONS

After his death, Tom and I had signs from our son. A cardinal in the yard chirping and staring at us for long periods of time, and pennies and dimes found in random locations. A sense of someone in the room or the smell of Alec's natural essence. However, I had never experienced anything from the afterlife like our sessions with a psychic medium. As a scientist, I had never been to a medium before. Our sessions made me a believer in the validity of mediumship. There was no way for them to know the things about our loved ones they did. It also confirmed my faith in the afterlife. I had three sessions with three different psychic mediums before I started writing this book, each one better and more validating than the last. My loved ones on the other side stepped forward to communicate with us, as did our son, and these communications from the afterlife are important to understand in the context of this book.

For the curious, I have detailed the three psychic medium sessions below. These sessions may shed additional light on my experience.

First psychic medium session:

Our first psychic medium session occurred almost by happenstance. Lexi, our ten-year-old dog, had surgery for cancer two and a half months after our son's death, and not long before my husband Tom and I had booked a bird sighting trip to Panama. I couldn't leave Lexi, so I stayed home with her while she was recovering. On Tom's flight from Miami to Panama City, a lady was sitting next to him in what would have been my seat . She had attended a retreat led by a quantum physicist on meditation and healing. They started talking, and Tom shared about Alec's death. She insisted that we have a session with the medium in South Africa who helped her tremendously after her sister passed away. She even paid for our session.

This first session in February after Alec passed was indeed helpful. The psychic medium was personable and easy to talk to, despite our being nervous. She used her gift of clairsentience to communicate with those who had passed. This means that she picked up on the emotions of spirits. As we had never been to a psychic medium before, she began the session by explaining that spirits in the spiritual realm are all around us and connected to everything from the trees and flowers to the mountains and ocean. When a human passes, they no longer have their physical body with all the medical conditions and aches and pains. Instead, they feel complete bliss, unconditional love, and happiness. They are free from all the physical and mental challenges that they had as a human being. During the video conference session, a close friend's father who had recently passed came forward, as did both of Tom's parents and my father. We were incredulous, because the medium brought up details that would be impossible for her to know, such as Tom surf fishing with his father on weekends during his childhood, and Alec wearing a patch on his eye as an infant and toddler to keep from going blind in one eye.

The medium was told that our parents were looking for 'someone to bring in'. We held our breath through a period of silence, hoping it would be Alec. When Alec started communicating with the medium, he sent fond family memories that no one would know except us. For example, she asked us about a special day in February, and we indicated we adopted him on February 15th and had always celebrated his Gotcha (Adoption) Day as a very special day. My hope soared. This was truly a communication with our son! No one outside of our family would know that date! I continued to hold my breath, hoping for more.

Alec sent memories of riding his bicycle and scooter around our old neighborhood. I let my breath go and took in a deep one. Tears were streaming down my face as I listened to these precious memories coming through. I glanced at Tom and could see he felt the same. Sad and confused, but happy that we were connected to him. I knew it was truly Alec, and while it was hard to believe, I grasped and held onto these precious memories as hard as I could.

One of the reasons I wanted to participate in a medium session was to find out if Alec was ok. I worried about him so much when he was alive because of his high functioning autism (formerly Asperger's) and attention deficit hyperactivity disorder (ADHD). The medium told us he is more than ok. He's happy and blissful and no longer struggles with the things he struggled with in his physical life. It touched my heart when he communicated that he understood that in putting up boundaries, we were only trying to help him, not control him, out of love. Most importantly to us, he knew we were good parents and did everything we could for him. He was going to keep going on that same path he had chosen until an overdose of some kind happened. We knew his death was an overdose, but at this point, had not received the medical examiner's report and did not know what substance caused his death. Alec also communicated that he wanted us to focus on ourselves now and have fun. He knew we had focused on him so much in the past years and it was our time now to enjoy each other and our own lives.

He also mentioned his sister, Vera, and that he knew that their strained relationship was because of him. He hoped Vera would be happy. He wished that things could have been different, and that Tom didn't have to experience the trauma of finding him. He stressed he didn't want that to be Tom's last memory of him. The medium stated that in his physical life, Alec had always felt different and not connected with others. Now he was feeling very connected with others and with All Things. This was extremely reassuring to me as a mother.

This medium mentioned someone whose name started with a "J", but we couldn't figure out who that might be. While we weren't prepared with questions to ask, we were convinced that it was Alec that the medium had connected with, and we were glad to know that he was happy.

Second psychic medium session:

My second psychic medium session was in person, and I participated without Tom. It was held in early November, a little over a year after Alec passed. I wanted to see if the experience would be different if I was alone, and I had suggested to Tom that we also set up a session for him. I was also curious to see if an in-person experience would be different from a virtual one. The medium was located in Wilmington, in a small studio behind her home. She was personable and with a bubbly personality, and this time I was more excited than nervous about the session.

The medium began the session with silence, then quickly stated that I had a lot of 'people'. My grandmother, Mama Mac, was standing right beside me with Pop behind her. Mama Mac wanted me to know that the entire family surrounded Alec and welcomed him home when he passed. That they had him and he was good. The medium told me that Mama Mac then came around in front of me and put her hand on my shoulder and said, "Not to worry, it's all going to be ok." Unfortunately, I didn't sense a thing.

Alec communicated much during this session. He was excited to be learning a lot about everything: about how things were connected, how things worked, the physical side and afterlife as well as our family. He wasn't sorry for anything because he was put in a physical body to have the specific experience that he had, to learn and to grow. The medium speculated that it was possible that he had judged someone about drug abuse in a prior life.

Alec's time on earth was predestined to be short this time, and he died when he was supposed to die. He had no pain when he died; instead, it was 'poof', and he was on the other side. He wished that he could have had the experience that he was supposed to have without hurting us. Alec communicated he had been depressed, lonely and isolated toward the end of his physical life, and that he did drugs to try to rise above that, to feel high, to feel joy. Now he has joy without the drugs.

He was happy we adopted him as it was meant to be. He knew we loved him, and he communicated some happy memories of the two of us, like making brownies with me one afternoon. Now he is happy and with family and ancestors.

The medium said, "In fact, he and your dad are walking on the beach right now. They're best buddies. Your dad is learning from Alec and watching out for him." My grandmother also made it a point to show that they were near a very large body of water. I assumed that was the beach since that was where we were at the time. The medium told me that Alec had visited us at our house immediately after he passed, but we hadn't sensed that he was there.

The medium asked about the significance of a lock, and I explained the police had to break the door down at Alec's apartment after he passed because the deadbolt was engaged.

Alec communicated it was very cool in the afterlife and that he was a teacher. He no longer had the awkwardness with social interactions or any other symptoms of Asperger's. He knew I would be proud of him because he is respected and known by many souls. He was dressed in a brown turtleneck and dark blue pants, ready to attend a concert. Music was playing in the background, a steady beat sounding like an electrical synthesizer, like Alec used to listen to when he studied.

This was the first time I heard about school in heaven, or at least classes, because none of it is mandatory. It's for the pleasure of learning. Alec asked the medium to tell me, "See, Mom. You don't have to stagnate here by not learning." That had real significance to me because I said it all the time after I retired. Alec communicated he was 'off doing his own thing' a lot while learning because he was more advanced, but that he was very happy. He studied at a level where few others were, but then he would be with family.

He hears us when we talk to him. He is hoping that we can 'hear him' although it is more likely that words or images would pop into our heads. I asked the medium how we would know that he was communicating. She said, "It will come in a dream or another way. If nothing else, you can always ask a medium to help you."

Alec said, "We could learn together."

I said, "I would love that, Alec."

"I will be here when you come, Mom, waiting for you. I can't wait to show you and Dad what it's like in heaven."

Through the medium, Alec let us know how much he liked the way Aunt Kathy had decorated the urn with his ashes with artificial flowers, to replicate the live flowers at his service. He also liked the tiny replica that we had at the beach.

This medium also mentioned someone very important with a "J" name. This medium was not aware of the other medium bringing this up. We still were not sure what this meant.

Third psychic medium session:

I met briefly with the last psychic medium, Tiffany, before scheduling the session because a colleague had suggested that the two of us needed to meet. We had a great conversation, and I mentioned I was interested in writing a book about Alec's struggles with addiction and our experience the first year after his death. The medium immediately said, "That sounds great, but I think the book should be from Alec's perspective. Let his voice be heard from the afterlife." This intrigued me and I couldn't let go of the thought.

She also suggested in this introductory meeting that I think about someone with a "J" name, possibly Joshua, because it was very strongly coming through as someone important to our son. Still, we could not think of anyone we knew named Joshua who had passed, despite all three mediums mentioning it. It was only two weeks later, in early November, that I had an excellent session with Tiffany. I learned a great deal from her. She saw things unfold like a movie coming through to her. Initially, our nephew's mother-in-law came through and wanted to give me somewhat of a warning not to carry so much grief around with me, as it can greatly affect my health.

Alec came forward hesitantly in this session, possibly because I had reached out to him less than a week earlier. He conveyed that the conversations about his death and circumstances were difficult.

The medium noted that he had been musically talented but didn't discipline himself that way. I remembered his piano lessons being a wash, but he had been told he had perfect pitch along the way. Alec communicated to her that in the afterlife, there were sounds and notes that you couldn't hear on earth with the physical ear. And magnificent colors in heaven that weren't seen on the physical side. He also communicated that God is so much more all-encompassing than what he had ever understood. There were days on the physical side when he was a little angry with God because he felt so alone. He hadn't realized how much God could fill that void with His love.

Alec had cherished moments in his physical life. He met a girlfriend in California at transition camp for those on the spectrum, and they became close. He bought his own car, and he had a family that loved him. There were painful moments too, like what happened in May before he passed. There was a car wreck. The sky was dark. He had stopped at a liquor store and was drinking out of the bottle. He ran into a telephone pole and totaled his new car. Luckily, no one was hurt.

Alec noted that there are a lot of fears that I hang on to but don't acknowledge, and that I tend to use the scapegoat of losing contact with him to replace all those other fears. He said it's not healthy for me to keep reaching out to him and burying so many fears under this umbrella. The medium counted at least eighteen fears that I need to acknowledge and let go. I knew I had a lot of fears and I'd always had anxiety. Some of those fears were that everything would fall apart, or that I would lose my husband or my daughter, especially since we lost our son. I was especially afraid of losing contact with Alec now that I had connected with him. I was realizing how much those fears were driving my life and my choices.

Tiffany suggested I make this part of the writing process after making a list of everything that I know I'm afraid of. She thought that would help with my fear of losing contact with him. Alec communicated he was able to play out his story in this life in a way that I was able to take it, given all those fears I had.

I asked if he knew about my conversations with the professors at the University of North Carolina about the experiment of a new technology to treat addictive tendencies.

He said, 'Mom thinks I'm God now!' That got some chuckles from Tiffany and me.

He then added, "I don't hear all her conversations, only when she calls on me." He then communicated that he liked the idea of me collaborating with researchers on transcranial alternating electrical current brain stimulation (tACS) for the treatment of addiction or substance use disorders (SUDs). He is happy we are going to pursue collaboration with researchers on it.

I asked about the day he died. The medical examiner's report stated that he died of kratom toxicity, and he communicated he didn't know kratom overdose was possible. Neither did Tiffany. He took more than the normal dose, but it had also interacted with something else. When he realized that something was wrong, it was too late, and he laid down, thinking he was taking a rest. He gave no cry for help, and he wasn't upset, nor did he feel pain. There was afternoon light coming through, so between two and four in the afternoon was likely when he laid down to rest. Then he was out of his body as a soul.

I then asked who Joshua was and noted that the two other mediums had also mentioned a 'J' name. Initially, Tiffany asked whether I had experienced a miscarriage or another birth, wondering if it could be a lost child. I told her I had experienced a miscarriage when we were going through fertility treatments. She noted I had grief wrapped up in that and that a part of me felt responsible for that.

"Is it true that you fear you are the reason that your babies have died?" she asked. I responded that I have wondered about that on occasion. Tiffany said, "That is not your fault. That is one of your fears—the potential that you could have caused the death of a child. Look into your inner child – love her. That innocent child is you. You did not cause the death of your child. Don't carry that grief, it will kill you. Don't carry that forward."

Both Alec and Tiffany told me, "You should let go of everything you fear, especially the part of you that is afraid of the true you. You're afraid that things are going to fall apart. That comes from somewhere and it could be a topic for another session." I eventually scheduled a psychic session with Tiffany two months later, after I had a draft of the book completed.

During this same session, I asked what Alec was teaching in heaven. Tiffany saw desks in a row, like a mirror within a mirror within a mirror (an infinity mirror) but with desks in each one. So many lives, so many lessons, so many teachers, so many students. Alec communicated he was teaching about how to see God in yourself and how to align with your true inner self. Alec sent the image of a frog that becomes prince, a metaphor for an undesirable character, finally embracing his kingly side. The issue of masculinity was and still is important to Alec, and now he is a strong leader and respected.

"It is nothing you caused and nothing society did to him." Tiffany said, referring to his need to feel masculine. "It is a mirror of the heart. He likes the man he sees in the mirror now."

At the end of this session, I again asked about the "J" name, as all three of the mediums had brought it up. Tiffany was clearly getting

'Joshua'. She didn't get anything directly from Alec, but she did say that the Hebrew name for Jesus (Yeshua) and Joshua (Yeshua or Jeshua), both short for Yehoshua (Jehoshua), were the same. I do believe that this is who was prominently coming through in our sessions.

During this last medium session, my son and Tiffany suggested I should not only write this book, but that it should be written every day for six weeks, or until it is complete. It wouldn't be until much later in transcendental conversations that I would find out why. Alec suggested I write early in the morning, when the veil between the physical and spiritual world is thinnest. He expressed he was honored and excited to help with the writing of this book. He wanted to share his journey and what he experienced in the afterlife, and he saw the book possibly helping human beings uncover their purpose on this earth, to learn and experience and, most of all, to love.

QUESTION & ANSWER
WITH ALEC

During some of our conversations, there were random questions from me to Alec that didn't fit into the flow of this book. I have included them here in case others have the same curiosity.

"Do you see animals there?"

I meet up with Bucky and Lexi sometimes. But I don't see them wandering around usually. It's when I think of them. I told you they are on a separate plane or dimension usually.

"Are there 'prehistoric' animals in the afterlife? Like dinosaurs?"

Yes, but they are not to be feared. They are spirits of mammals that lived on earth long ago. They do not need to hunt and kill for food. So they are good and loving.

"When you visit the animals, can you play with the leopards and cheetah? Pet them? You said it was safe?"

Yes, it is safe. And we connect with their souls, not physically pet them. It's fascinating to connect with them because they have seen so much in their prior lives.

"What about grass and trees and plants? They are living, are they not?"

They live on earth, but they have group souls. So each species of tree has a soul and not multiple souls. Plants do as well. You haven't seen grass and trees in the visions I have sent you, only because they haven't been in some of the afterlife views that I've sent, but they are in many of the views I've seen. It's all about the different dimensions. There are many dimensions, and it is impossible to tap them all or share them all with you.

"Do you explore different places on earth too, or just the universes?"

Not anymore. I did at first, but there is so much to see on the spiritual side. And we have a good sense as to what is there from living our physical lives and being around our living loved ones. Remember that we have memories from all our past lives too, plus our ancestors' lives.

"Have you seen jewels? Or jewel-like structures on living things like grass or leaves?"

I have seen grass that looks like it is made of colored ice, glistening in the light. I have seen leaves that look similar. But I haven't seen jewels. That doesn't mean they aren't around. I am early on my eternal journey.

"Have you seen streets of gold?"

That sounds like something we would find near the higher beings. I've a long way to go before I can enter that dimension, closer to the higher beings and closer to God. I need to be pure and all love.

"Do you feel wind there, Alec? It is windy today at the beach."

That's funny to think about, Mom. The wind blowing spirits around since we are balls of light. Like a pinball machine!

"Ha ha! Yes, that is kind of funny."

I only get the sense of gentle breeze occasionally. I've not seen strong winds like you get in what you call a squall or storm. Those happen on earth and in other planetary systems, but we don't necessarily experience them.

"What about rain or snow?"

There is rain at times. Remember that we exist in constant light unless we are in your physical realm as spirits. The weather doesn't bother us as souls. We don't get wet or blown away. I've always actually really liked the rain. Steady rain. It's calming. I have seen snow only on my visits to the physical side. Because we are in the past, present and future simultaneously, there can be snow in some of those dimensions.

"I can't believe I'm talking about the weather with the soul of my deceased son."

Yeah, it's like when you talk to your mother. It's one of the first things you and Nana always talk about. The weather there and where you are.

"Yep. I was thinking the same thing. She grew up on a dairy farm, so the weather was very important to them."

I know, Mom. Remember, I can read your mind!

"Do souls laugh and have a sense of humor? I bet you get along really well if they do. You always had such a great sense of humor, Alec."

Of course. We all laugh and kid around. It is part of the sense of bliss here to laugh and be happy. Otherwise, being serious and somber all the time would be suffocating. We especially do that in our soul groups and with our relatives and family.

"Do you ever sit in the clouds, Alec? Why do I have a vision of your spirit, sitting in a cloud, looking down on earth?"

It may appear that I am sitting in a cloud, but you know that's not possible, right? I am a ball of energy, of light. And a cloud is only an accumulation of moisture. If I tried to sit on it, I'd fall right through it.

"Do spirits create forms of life other than reincarnating? If they do, how do they do that?"

I cannot say. Perhaps they do at higher levels than I am. The creator is the one who creates most forms of life, at least intelligent life. So creating forms of life would likely involve God and possibly higher beings.

"Are there different worlds in the afterlife? A world to get to know the true self? A world of creation and non-creation? A world of All Knowing? The world of altered time? What are they and when do souls visit those worlds? Is there a simulated earth?"

There are different worlds in the afterlife. I can't explain them, but there is a world that newer souls go to that helps them learn about their true self. Any spirit can go there and refresh and learn, especially after a new physical experience. There are other worlds, one of which involves an earth-like place that we can go to and just be. When we go to earth, we are living and trying to experience, even though the physical body we inhabit doesn't necessarily know the intention of learning. It can be difficult for us. This earth-like world is intended to allow us to experience earthly things without having to try so hard to learn.

"So it's a vacation for spirits?"

Yeah, I guess you could say that.

"Are there souls that are completely dedicated to earth and what is going on there? How much control do they have? Can they alter events?"

While we all watch over loved ones, there are souls who are specifically watching over earth. They don't stay in the spirit realm but rather are constantly in the physical world and they live and exist on earth to watch over what is happening there.

"Who do they communicate with? Are they supposed to report back to someone or something? What are they reporting on?"

They communicate with spirit guides and teachers, and they report what is going on in the physical world with politics, wars, destruction of earth's resources, hate crimes, all the terrible things that are happening. They also report on positive things but the negative sort of overwhelms right now.

ACKNOWLEDGEMENTS

The artwork on the front cover was painted by Stefan Senna, who inspired me through his paintings of his perceptions of heaven based on his two near-death experiences (NDEs). I cannot thank my close friend Sallie Williams enough. She helped me with so many aspects of publishing, including design and layout of the cover and entire book. She is always there for me. An excellent graphics designer, it's amazing how she can turn mediocre-looking text into something brilliant.

I would like to acknowledge Hope Mueller, who I met when we both consulted with the same client. She managed to rope me into agreeing to write a chapter in her book at the same time I was writing this book, and she has somehow managed to inspire me and change my life since I met her. I appreciate her advice on publishing a book and holding my hand along the way. Hope is an amazing editor and gave me excellent advice for restructuring the book to make the story flow.

I am grateful to Hope for introducing me to Tiffany Harelik, founder of Wiseskies Collective and renowned medium, who inspired me to start and complete this book in record time. I had never even heard of automatic writing, but once I tried it, I was a believer. I am also grateful for the practical advice from Tiffany on my approach and formatting of dialogue. I am thankful for the two mediums I saw before I met Tiffany. Each one gave me hope and new understanding.

My mother's compassion and prayers for me have given me strength throughout my life, and especially since Alec's death. I wish my father, who passed two years before Alec, could read these pages, but I am glad that he and Alec are together and can hang out together. My sister is always there for me and my family, even when mad at me for getting on her case. Thank you for being my close friend and my sister. I hope my brother can appreciate this book and remember the times we tried time travel long ago. My husband's cousin John Evans and his wife Nurisell Nuñez, our nephew and his wife Andrew and Florencia Girman, have given us tremendous family support with Alec and Vera before and since Alec's death. I also thank all the rest of my relatives and ancestors, living and passed, that gave me support and love, and most of all, believed in me throughout my lifetime. Each one of you is a part of who I am. I am happy that those of you who have already passed were there to embrace and surround Alec with love and welcome him home.

My close friends are my lifeline. I am fortunate to have many high school (Sallie Williams, Ethel Lucius, Susan Butler, Lee Ann Calhoun and Nancy Cunnane) and college friends (Becky Brooks, Cheryl Hartsoe, Lisa Kolb, Nancy Cohn, Paige Boyette, Allison Laing, Liz Selisker, Kim Woodard) that are each still very much an anchor for me. My graduate school, work colleague and close friend, Kathy Harris, always has my back. I feel I can call on these friends for almost anything. Other friends, such as Cappy Hagman, Annie McNeill, Diane Catellier, Chris Kolman and Nina Ranieri also gave me support. All these friends have been there for me throughout the years of Alec's worsening addiction, and I clung to them after his death. I gained strength from all of them, and they were all there for me. The closeness we have and the laughter, despite sadness, has helped keep me sane.

Colleagues and collaborators such as Mary Beth Ritchey, Michele Jonsson-Funk, Thomas Rhodes, Susan Hartmaier, Molly Aldridge, Kristy Iglay, Katie Brind-Amour and others held me up and covered for me while I was in the early grieving stages, and I will always remember that with gratitude. I simply can't name them all, but this support system is such a good feeling for someone who stresses about asking anyone for anything.

Close friends Ethel Lucius, Cheryl Hartsoe and Kathy Harris gave me tremendous encouragement and important initial input as early readers. I appreciate their honest feedback, as this was a book very different from those they typically enjoy. I am incredibly grateful to my other early readers: Rachel Leahy, Betsy Gornet and Trish Snoots. All the early readers gave very useful feedback to help me improve the readability of the book.

Our daughter, Vera, is an inspiration. We are so proud of her for the person she has become and her passion for what she believes in. I hope she grabs everything she can out of life! We love her more than she can imagine. We appreciate her acknowledging rather than suppressing her feelings about her brother's death. She gave me constructive, thoughtful suggestions, which I incorporated into the book.

I could not have gotten through the year following our son's death without my husband, Tom. He has given me immeasurable support and encouragement over the thirty years that I have known him. He has always been my strongest fan and believed in me as my best friend and life partner. I love him more than I can express. This book was painful for him, and I respected that. Yet he found it in him to read it many times and give me feedback as well as actively edit the text. This journey has been intense emotionally, and he has been my rock as I think I have for him.

Alec communicated during the medium session with Tiffany that he didn't want his father to feel left out of the book writing and asked if we could include one of his bird or animal photographs. However, Tom contributed significantly to the book by being one of my readers, supporting me while I was writing, and helping me remember the facts during emotional times. He also helped me choose the title and the artwork for the cover of the book, and he wrote and edited many of the chapters. His handprints are all over this book.

Love is everything. I hope that by reading this book, readers recognize that and appreciate that life does not end when our physical body gives out. We have much to look forward to and much to do before then. Also that there are ways to continue your relationship with your loved ones who pass to the spiritual realm, only in a different way.

Praise be to the God and Father of our Lord Jesus Christ, the Father of compassion and the God of all comfort, who comforts us in all our troubles, so that we can comfort those in any trouble with the comfort we ourselves have received from God.

2 Corinthians 1:3-4

The Holy Bible, New International Version® NIV®

Copyright © 1973, 1978, 1984, 2011 by Biblica, Inc®

YOU'RE THE GHOST

By Donna Ashworth

There's a part of the grieving process,
where your soul kind of leaves your body too.
As though it's off searching for the one you lost,
somewhere in the ether.

You walk around,
doing all the right things,
putting one foot in front of the other,
living,
but it's really as though you're the ghost.

Perhaps you are.
Perhaps your soul searches,
until you find the one you miss,
and they tell you to go back and live.

So, when that numbness passes brave one,
maybe it's time to do what you are told,
go back and live,
twice as hard.

You don't belong there in the ether,
nor do you need to search for the one you lost,
they find you.
And when they do, you'll feel it.

From Ashworth, Donna. Sunday Times Bestseller: <u>I Wish I Knew.</u> Black & White Publishing, 2022.

ABOUT THE AUTHOR

Cindy Girman is founder and leader of a consulting firm that works with pharmaceutical companies on ways to generate more efficient and meaningful evidence on how medicines work. She holds a Doctor of Public Health in biostatistics with emphasis in epidemiology from University of North Carolina (UNC) and is a fellow of the International Society of Pharmacoepidemiology. Cindy and her husband are collaborating with researchers at UNC on non-pharmacological transcranial alternating current stimulation of the brain as a treatment for substance use disorder, a keen interest of theirs.

Cindy and Tom enjoy travel, especially safari and exotic bird watching, and spending time with friends and family. The author was raised in western North Carolina, and she and Tom split their time between the coast and mountains. Alec was raised in Raleigh and Chapel Hill, North Carolina. They are incredibly proud of their daughter Vera, a fashion photographer and art director for photoshoots.

After administrative costs, 50% of the proceeds from this book will be directed to addiction research.

Photography by Vera Karine
Illustration by Stefan Senna
Cover design by Sallie Williams

www.wingsofpeacepress.com

www.ingramcontent.com/pod-product-compliance
Lightning Source LLC
Chambersburg PA
CBHW020442130626
46549CB00001B/271